The

Cookbook

by Debbie Wells

Cover art: Arthur Often
Cover photography: Cindy Fiore (top) and Ann Ehringhaus
(bottom)
Cover and text design: Michael McOwen
Editorial assistance: Jolene Robinson

Published by
The Back Porch Restaurant
P.O. Box 420
Ocracoke, North Carolina 27960

Fifth Printing: July 2003

ISBN 0-9632258-0-4
Library of Congress Catalogue
Card Number 92-90107

Manufactured in the United States of America

Dedicated with love to

my father, Irby Gorman

my mother, Elizabeth Gorman

and

my grandmother, Lola Turner

Table of Contents

Salads

Entrees

Breads

Desserts

Basics and Helpful Tips

The Back Porch Restaurant opened its doors in February of 1984. My husband, John, and I named the restaurant in honor of our huge, screened porch dining room. Summertime, screened porches, and good food just naturally seemed to go together.

You will find us nestled in a grove of cedar trees in the small island village of Ocracoke located on the southernmost tip of North Carolina's Outer Banks. If you decide to take a trip to Ocracoke, make plans to stay a few days. We're a long way from everywhere, accessible only by ferry, and not the kind of place you'll be anxious to leave.

We serve dinner seven nights a week and are open from mid-April through mid-October. Our menu offers a wide range of possibilities, with a strong emphasis on natural, wholesome ingredients and the many types of fresh seafood for which the Outer Banks are famous. We bake our own bread, offer a different homemade soup every night, and feature a variety of dazzling desserts, all created from scratch.

This book is the result of many happy years in the kitchen, and is in response to hundreds of requests for recipes. It is affectionately offered in the belief that good food, like love, is meant to be shared.

I was raised in a family where food reigned supreme. Both my parents grew up on small, self-sufficient, family farms in rural Georgia. As children they played in cornfields, helped my grandparents make sorghum syrup, and took trips to the local mill where their cornmeal was ground. Vegetables were beans, tomatos, and peas, or whatever else they could grow, bacon came from the pig who was yesterday's pet, and the only nuts in the world were peanuts and pecans. Providing food for the family was a full-time job, and mealtime was serious business.

By the time my sisters and I came along in the early 1950's, my mom and dad had taken to the suburbs of Atlanta. Although food was easier to come by, their attitudes remained much the same. If we were not at the table, you could bet that somebody, somewhere, was preparing to be. Whether actually in the kitchen or just "working up an appetite" as my dad used to say, the next meal was always foremost in our minds. Our enthusiasm was fostered not only by the exceptional technical abilities of my mother, who was and is a remarkable southern cook, but also by the consistent and regular devotion which she applied to her work. She believed wholeheartedly in giving her family three meals a day, served punctually, with everyone present and accounted for. The dinner hour took priority over all other activities, gave structure to our lives, and brought the family together in one common purpose.

Today, we're scattered up and down the East Coast, and food remains the most joyful of all the ties that bind us. We take great pleasure in cooking for one another on our frequent family visits, and haul gifts of local specialities across state lines. My grandmother, now elderly and unable to cook for herself, still loves to share recipes, talk at length about the food she ate as a child, and complain vehemently when she's served something that's not up to snuff. Both my sisters are professional chefs and we swap recipes, compare notes, and exchange ideas. Mom still spends hours in her kitchen entertaining family and friends and cooking for my dad and every night at six, regular as clockwork, they sit down to their evening meal. As for me, well, I just count my blessings and look forward to those nights when I can walk into Mom's kitchen, pull up a chair, and sit down too.

Appetizers

When I was child, my family would spend two weeks every summer in Daytona Beach. One of the highlights of the trip would be going out to eat at a seaside restaurant and ordering a shrimp cocktail before dinner. It was one of the few times throughout the year that my sisters and I were allowed such indulgences. We relished every mouthful, enchanted by the tiny forks, the little cups of sauce, and the dainty stemmed glasses.

This fondness for small, fanciful portions is apparently part of our collective unconscious. In the last twenty years, the appetizer has enjoyed unprecedented popularity, with many chefs devoting half of their menus to this genre. Far from its original role as an opener to a meal, the appetizer has moved to the fore. Enhanced by a salad, a bowl of soup, and dessert, we can experience an ever-broader range of ingredients and preparations.

Crab Beignets

We developed this recipe for our first menu nine years ago and it continues to be our top selling appetizer. At first glance, this preparation may appear a bit complicated. However, by preparing the Mustard Sauce and Crepe Shells a day ahead, the last minute preparation is greatly simplified.

1 pound cooked and ready to use claw meat
from the Atlantic blue crab
1 pound cream cheese, room temperature
1 Tbs. worchestershire sauce
1 Tbs. fresh, minced garlic
1 tsp. dried tarragon leaves
1 recipe Crepe Shells, see page 182
1 recipe Beignet Batter, recipe follows
1 recipe Mustard Sauce, recipe follows

1) Pick through crabmeat, discarding any bits of shell and pressing out excess water.

2) Cream together remaining ingredients and stir in crabmeat, mixing thoroughly.

3) Place crepe shell on work surface, pale side up, and place 3 Tbs. or about 2 ounces crab filling in the center. Roll crepe around filling as one would fold a letter. Tuck ends under to form a small packet. Refrigerate until ready to fry. Beignets may be prepared up to six hours in advance.

4) To fry beignets, prepare Beignet Batter. Heat deep fryer to 350° or fill large heavy skillet with frying oil to a depth of 1 inch. Heat until almost smoking.

5) Dip beignet into batter, coating evenly, and immediately add to hot frying oil. Cook until golden and crispy, turning once. Remove from oil onto paper towels and blot excess oil.

6) Serve immediately with Mustard Sauce on the side and lemon wedges.

Approximately 16 beignets.

Beignet Batter

2 cups plain white flour
4 Tbs. cornstarch
2 tsp. baking powder
1 tsp. salt
4 whole eggs
2 egg yolks
4 tsp. dark sesame oil
2 cups cold water
oil for frying

1) Combine dry ingredients in a large mixing bowl and mix together with a balloon whisk.

2) Combine wet ingredients in a medium mixing bowl and whisk together with a balloon whisk.

3) Pour wet ingredients into dry and fold together lightly with a rubber spatula until barely mixed. Batter will be lumpy and rough.

Yields about 4 cups.

Mustard Sauce

1/2 cup mayonnaise
1/3 cup Dijon mustard
1/2 tsp. worchestershire sauce
1/2 tsp. lemon juice
1 dash tabasco

1) Blend all ingredients thoroughly. Refrigerate until ready to use.

Yield 1 cup.

Back Porch Seafood Paté with Lemon Cream

1 8-cup capacity mold or 2 4-cup capacity molds. Spray with Pam and line molds with saran wrap, smoothing sides.

1 gallon lightly salted water
1 pound shrimp, peeled, deveined, and rinsed
1 pound scallops, rinsed well
1 pound fish fillets, skin, bone, and dark flesh
    removed, rinsed
2 Tbs. vegetable oil
1 Tbs. minced, fresh garlic
1 cup diced onion
1 pound butter, at cool room temperature
1 tsp. salt or more to taste
4 tsp. fresh lemon juice
1/3 tsp. paprika
1/2 tsp. dried basil leaves
2 dashes Tabasco sauce
dash nutmeg
2 Tbs. tomato paste
6 ounces heavy cream
3/4 cup chopped parsley

1) Divide gallon of water into 2 soup pots and bring to a simmer over medium heat. Add shrimp to first pot of water. Combine fish and scallops and add to second pot.

2) Gently poach seafood until firm throughout. Pour shrimp into colander, straining off liquid. Cool to room temperature. Repeat with fish and scallops, keeping separate from shrimp. Cool to room temperature. Cooking liquids may be saved for other uses.

3) Process shrimp in food processor fitted with a metal blade until finely ground. Place in medium mixing bowl. Process fish and scallops in food processor until finely ground. Place in second medium mixing bowl.

4) Heat 2 Tbs. vegetable oil in medium sauté pan and sauté garlic and onions until soft but not brown. Place a third of the cooked onions in bowl with shrimp. Place remaining cooked onions in bowl with fish and scallops. Cool completely.

5) To bowl of shrimp and onions, add 1/3 pound butter, 1/4 tsp. salt, 2 tsp. lemon juice, 1/3 tsp. paprika, 1/2 tsp. basil, dash of Tabasco, 2 Tbs. tomato paste, and 4 Tbs. heavy cream. Blend thoroughly with a rubber spatula and process again in food processor until smooth. Taste and adjust salt, if necessary. Spoon into bottom of mold smoothing top. Chill while proceeding with next step.

6) To bowl of fish and scallops, add 2/3 pound butter, 3/4 tsp. salt, 2 tsp. lemon juice, dash Tabasco, dash nutmeg, and 8 Tbs. heavy cream. Blend thoroughly with rubber spatula and process again in food processor until smooth. Taste and adjust salt, if necessary. Spoon half of this mixture into mold on top of shrimp, smoothing with spatula. Refrigerate mold again and return remaining puree to food processor adding 3/4 cup chopped parsley. Process a third and final time until parsley is just blended into mixture. Spoon into mold over white scallop and fish layer and smooth top. Refrigerate 8 hours or overnight or freeze for up to a week. (Thaw overnight in refrigerator.) When thoroughly chilled, invert onto serving platter, remove saran wrap, and garnish as desired. Pass Lemon Cream separately or spoon over paté just before serving. Serve with crackers or toasted bread rounds.

Serves 15-20 people

Lemon Cream
1 cup heavy cream
1/4 tsp. salt
dash black pepper
1/2 tsp. fresh, minced garlic
2 Tbs. fresh lemon juice
2 egg yolks

1) Combine cream, salt, pepper, garlic, and lemon juice in a small saucepan. Heat gently until almost simmering.
2) Put egg yolks in a medium mixing bowl and whisk lightly. Slowly add half the scalded cream to the yolks, whisking constantly, then return all to the saucepan. Stir gently over low heat until hot to the touch and slightly thickened. Chill thoroughly before serving.

Yields about one cup.

Sesame Shrimp on Wilted Greens

This recipe came to us through my sister Sharon, who got it fom her friend Johnny O'Neal of West Palm Beach, Florida (no relation to the Ocracoke O'Neals), who got it from somebody else. If you're the person who originally created this wonderful dish, thanks alot. Our customers love it.

1 pound fresh spinach, stemmed and rinsed
1/2 gallon lightly salted water
4 Tbs. dark sesame oil
4 tsp. soy sauce or tamari
4 tsp. fresh, minced ginger root
4 tsp. fresh, minced garlic
20 medium shrimp, peeled, deveined, rinsed
   and patted dry
1 tsp. sesame seeds, lightly toasted

1) Bring water to a boil. Add spinach, stirring, until spinach is wilted and bright green. Remove from heat, drain well, chop coarsely, and set aside.

2) Heat oil gently in a medium sized sauté pan. Add soy, ginger root, garlic, and shrimp. Sauté over low heat until shrimp are pink and just cooked through.

3) Divide spinach equally between four salad plates. Place 5 shrimp on each bed of spinach and divide cooking juices equally over each portion.

4) Sprinkle with toasted sesame seeds and serve immediately.

Serves 4

Warm Terrine of Chevre

My sister Sharon, who loves chevre, was the inspiration for this dish. Use any type of fresh goat cheese for this recipe. The salt content of fresh chevres varies greatly, so, add salt to suit your taste.

Preheat oven to 400°

1 Tbs. olive oil
1/2 cup onion, diced fine
1/2 cup red bell pepper, diced fine
1/2 cup frozen leaf spinach, thawed, drained, and
   coarsely chopped or 1 cup fresh spinach,
   stemmed, rinsed, drained, and coarsely
   chopped. Pack firmly into measuring cup.
4 ounces cream cheese, room temperature
12 ounces fresh chevre, room temperature
salt to taste
1 24 inch long loaf of French bread, sliced into
   thin rounds.

1) Heat olive oil in large sauté pan. Add onions and red bell pepper and cook over medium heat until softened. Add spinach and continue to cook until spinach is wilted and all moisture is evaporated.

2) Reduce heat to low, add both cheeses, and stir to thoroughly blend. Add salt to taste. Cook over low heat, stirring often, until thoroughly warmed.

3) While cheese is heating, put sliced bread rounds on baking sheet and place in preheated 400° oven. Toast lightly.

4) Scoop cheese into a warmed 3 cup capacity souffle dish or ramekin. Serve immediately with warm, toasted bread rounds and knives for spreading.

Serves 8-10

Herbed Cream Cheese Spread

This recipe lends itself to a wide variety of adaptations. Emphasize one herb over another, add toasted pecans or walnuts, even sun dried tomatoes or black olives. For parties, dust a small tart pan or any 3 cup capacity mold with finely ground nuts and breadcrumbs. Then fill with cheese, chill, and unmold. We get raves on this presentation at parties. In the dining room, we serve this alongside our Smoked Carolina Bluefish, which is shipped to us weekly from Bentley's Smokehouse in Chapel Hill, North Carolina.

1 pound cream cheese, room temperature
1/4 pound butter, room temperature
4 tsp. fresh, minced garlic
1 tsp. fresh, minced shallots
4 tsp. dried or fresh dill weed
1 tsp. dried basil leaves or 1 Tbs.
fresh, chopped basil
1/2 tsp. coarsely ground black pepper
1/3 cup fresh, minced parsley

1) Cream together cream cheese and butter until fluffy.

2) Add all remaining ingredients and beat until thoroughly blended.

3) Pack in any 2 cup capacity ramekin or bowl and refrigerate until ready to serve.

4) Serve with crackers or toasted French bread rounds. Great with smoked fish or caviar.

Serves 6-8

Basil and Tomato Cheese Wheel

Spray the bottom of a 9-inch springform pan with Pam and line with parchment paper.

3 pounds cream cheese, room temperature
1/2 cup sun dried tomatoes packed in oil, pureed
1/2 pound chevre, room temperature
1 cup basil pesto, use your own recipe or see page 184

1) Cream 1 pound cream cheese with 1/2 cup sundried tomatoe puree. Salt to taste, if necessary, and smooth into the bottom of prepared pan.

2) Cream second pound of cream cheese with 1/2 pound chevre. Salt to taste, if necessary, and smooth over tomatoe layer.

3) Cream third pound of cream cheese with pesto. Salt to taste, if necessary, and smooth over chevre layer. Cover and chill thoroughly.

4) Run thin knife around inside of pan and remove cuff. Invert onto serving platter, peeling off paper. Garnish and serve with toasted bread or crackers.

Serves 20-30

Shrimp Breton

1 pound medium shrimp, peeled, deveined, rinsed,
* and patted dry*
8 to 10 5-inch long bamboo skewers
2 Tbs. olive oil
1 recipe Shrimp Breton Glaze, recipe follows
1 recipe Bacon Salad, recipe follows

1) Spear 4-6 shrimp onto each skewer.

2) Heat oil in large sauté pan, add kabobs and quickly cook, liberally basting all sides with Shrimp Breton Glaze. Remove when shrimp are pink and cooked through.

3) On individual plates, mound a spoonful of Bacon Salad and place glazed shrimp kabob on top. Serve with wedge of lemon.

Serves 8-10 as an appetizer course or 4-5 as a main course

Shrimp Breton Glaze
2 Tbs. vegetable oil
1 cup onions, finely diced
1 Tbs. fresh, minced garlic
1 28-ounce can crushed tomatoes in puree
1 small bay leaf
1/4 tsp. fennel seed
1 1/2 tsp. dried thyme leaves
1 1/2 tsp. dried oregano leaves
2 dashes cayenne pepper
1 tsp. chili powder
1/4 tsp. crushed red pepper flakes
1 tsp. paprika
1 tsp. salt
1/4 tsp. coarsely ground black pepper
1/4 cup red wine vinegar
1/4 cup molasses
1/4 cup worchestershire sauce

1/4 cup Dijon mustard
1 1/2 tsp. filé powder
1/4 cup fresh, chopped parsley
4 Tbs. unsalted butter, room temperature

1) Heat oil in large sauce pan, add onions and garlic. Cook until onions are soft.

2) Add all remaining ingredients, except for filé powder, parsley and butter.

3) Simmer uncovered for 20 minutes.

4) Remove from heat and stir in filé powder, parsley, and butter. (This sauce can be stored up to 3 weeks under refrigeration. It is great used as a barbecue sauce on just about anything.)

Yield 3 cups

Bacon Salad
1 pound bacon, chopped into 1/2 inch pieces
4 ripe tomatoes, peeled, seeded, and chopped fine
1/2 cup scallions, green part only, chopped
1/4 cup parsley, minced fine
1/2 tsp. salt
1/4 tsp. coarse black pepper
1/4 cup red wine vinegar
1/8 cup olive oil

1) Cook bacon over medium heat until crisp and brown. Remove bacon bits from fat with a slotted spoon. Put on paper towels and allow to cool. In a medium mixing bowl, combine bacon with all remaining ingredients and set aside. Discard bacon fat or retain for another use.

Yields about 3 cups

Shrimp Marinated in Dill and White Wine

1/2 gallon water
1/2 tsp. salt
1 bay leaf
2 pounds medium shrimp, in their shells
2/3 cup fresh lemon juice
1/2 cup dry white wine
4 tsp. dried or fresh dill weed, minced
1 Tbs. fresh, minced chives
1 tsp. fresh ground black pepper
1 tsp. salt
1/2 tsp. fresh, minced garlic
2 drops Tabasco sauce
2/3 cup virgin olive oil

1) Bring water, salt, and bay leaf to a boil in a large sauce pan.

2) Add shrimp and simmer gently until shrimp are pink and just cooked through.

3) Drain shrimp and allow to cool. Peel, leaving tails intact, and devein. Set aside.

4) In a medium mixing bowl combine lemon juice, white wine, dill, chives, pepper, salt, garlic, Tabasco, and olive oil. Whisk thoroughly, add shrimp and toss to coat shrimp evenly. Refrigerate for 5 hours.

5) To serve, remove shrimp from marinade with a slotted spoon and arrange on a decorative platter. Garnish as desired.

Serves 8 - 10

Shrimp with Lemon and Fresh Basil

1/2 gallon water
1/2 tsp. salt
1 bay leaf
4 lemon slices
2 pounds shrimp, in their shells
1 cup virgin olive oil
1/3 cup fresh lemon juice
1/2 tsp. salt
1 tsp. fresh, minced garlic
2 Tbs. fresh, minced basil leaves
2 Tbs. fresh, minced parsley
1/4 tsp. coarse black pepper

1) Combine water, salt, bay leaf, and lemon slices in a sauce pan over high heat. Simmer 3 minutes, then add shrimp. Lower heat and cook until shrimp are pink throughout.

2) Drain off water, allow shrimp to cool. Peel, leaving tails intact, and devein. Set aside.

3) Combine remaining ingredients in a medium mixing bowl, whisking until thoroughly blended. Add shrimp, toss to coat shrimp evenly and refrigerate 5 -6 hours.

4) To serve, remove shrimp from marinade with a slotted spoon and arrange on a decorative platter. Garnish as desired.

Serves 8 -10

Shrimp in Spicy Marinade

1 half gallon water
1/2 tsp. salt
1 tsp. dried thyme leaves
1 bay leaf
2 pounds shrimp, in their shells
2/3 cup ketchup
1/4 cup red wine vinegar
2 Tbs. worchestershire sauce
1 Tbs. honey
1 tsp. salt
1/2 tsp. dry mustard
2 dashes chili powder
1 1/2 tsp. fresh, minced garlic
4 Tbs. fresh, minced parsley
2/3 cup olive oil
5 paper thin slices purple onion,
  broken into rings.

1) Bring water, salt, thyme, and bay leaf to a boil in a large sauce pan set over high heat.

2) Reduce heat, add shrimp and cook gently until pink throughout.

3) Drain shrimp, allow to cool, and remove shells and veins, leaving tails intact.

4) Combine all remaining ingredients, except onions, in a medium mixing bowl and whisk until thoroughly blended.

5) Add onions and shrimp, toss to coat shrimp evenly, and refrigerate 6 hours.

6) To serve, remove shrimp and onions from marinade with a slotted spoon and arrange on a decorative platter.

Serves 8-10

Scallop Seviche

This is a zesty, spicy marinade of Spanish origin. The lime juice and salt chemically "cook" the scallops, giving them a unique texture and a tangy flavor. This is equally good using king mackerel, wahoo, dolphin, or any other firm game fish.

1/2 cup fresh lime juice
1/4 cup olive oil
1 Tbs. fresh or dried dill weed, chopped
2 tsp. salt
1 2-ounce jar pimiento, drained and chopped
1/2 cup scallions, sliced into small rings
1 pound fresh scallops, rinsed and patted dry,
  small, tough, side muscle removed and sliced
    crosswise, if thick.

1) In a medium mixing bowl, combine lime juice, olive oil, dill weed, salt, pimiento, and scallions.

2) Add scallops, toss to evenly coat with the marinade, cover, and refrigerate for 8-12 hours.

3) Remove the scallops, pimiento, and scallions from the marinade with a slotted spoon and mound onto serving plate lined with lettuce. Garnish with lime slices and pass Horseradish Sauce, see page 92, separately, if you like.

Serves 4

Debbie's Chicken Liver Paté with Green Peppercorns

Spray any 6 cup capacity decorative mold or loaf pan with Pam, then line with a sheet of saran wrap or wax paper cut to fit.

1/2 gallon lightly salted water
2 tsp. whole black peppercorns
1/2 tsp. ground all spice
3 bay leaves
3 sprigs fresh parsley
2 pounds fresh chicken livers, rinsed and drained
2 Tbs. olive oil
1 1/4 cup onion, diced fine
1 Tbs. fresh, minced garlic
1 egg, hard boiled and chopped
1/2 tsp. salt
2 tsp. dry mustard
1/2 tsp. nutmeg
1/2 tsp. ground allspice
1 tsp. dried rosemary leaves
1 tsp. dried thyme leaves
1/2 tsp. dried basil leaves
2 Tbs. fresh, minced parsley
1/4 cup brandy
2 Tbs. dry sherry
2 dashes Tabasco
1 pound unsalted butter, room temperature
1/2 cup heavy cream
4 Tbs. green peppercorns

1) Combine 1/2 gallon water, peppercorns, allspice, bay leaves, and parsley in large soup pot. Bring to a boil and simmer for 5 minutes. Strain, reserving water and discarding spices.

2) Return water to a boil, add chicken livers, and simmer gently until livers are firm and slightly pink in the center. Drain off liquid and allow livers to cool to room temperature. Place livers in bowl of food processor fitted with a metal blade and process into a smooth paste.

Scrape paste into a large mixing bowl and set aside.

3) Heat olive oil in a sauté pan, add onions and garlic, and cook until onions are soft. Add to livers along with chopped boiled egg and all spices. Stir well to incorporate.

4) Stir in brandy, sherry and Tabasco. Stir in butter in 2 or 3 additions, then cream and peppercorns. Correct salt. Spoon into prepared mold smoothing top. Refrigerate for 8 hours or overnight.

5) To serve, invert onto a decorative platter. Remove paper. Garnish as desired and serve with crackers or toasted French bread rounds and sweet gherkins.

Serves 15-20 people

Soups

The only homemade soup my mom ever makes is vegetable soup. She combines a jar of her own canned tomatoes with a little of the freshest summer corn, then adds limas, potatoes, onions, cabbage, and a little chicken stock. After a brief simmer, it's ready to eat. Next, she fries thin slices of "streak o' lean" until they're crisp and brown. These salty, chewy, baconlike squares are served on the side, with a batch of her melt-in-the-mouth white meal cornbread. For eighteen years, this was homemade soup. We had the usual Campbell's varieties for lunch, of course, and if we were sick, Campbell's chicken noodle, saltines and a Coke was the standard cure for anything that ailed us. But their was certainly no chance of confusing the two soups. Even at age six, I knew the difference between canned and homemade.

So, it may surprise you to learn that at the restaurant we use canned chicken broth as the liquid base for most of our soups. I know I'm supposed to be slaving over a stockpot, safeguarding all my vegetable ends for this one noble purpose, but I've never had much luck producing a hearty, full flavored, vegetable broth in large quantities. To make a meat flavored broth, one must have bones, and boning chicken breasts by the hundreds is no longer my idea of a good time. This is not to say that at home, with more time and different priorities, I don't make homemade broths. I do, particularly fish broths, because I love them, and those you can't buy. So if you have the time and the inclination, turn to the back of this chapter and find the recipes for stocks. But, if you have an hour to fix dinner, and a taste for soup and cornbread, give yourself a break. You can make almost any one of these recipes in half an hour and have the other half hour to sit down and relax.

Zucchini Soup with Sour Cream and Dill

4 Tbs. butter
6 cups chopped zucchini, about 4 medium sized
1 cup chopped onion
2 tsp. fresh, minced garlic
1/2 tsp. dried thyme leaves
1 bay leaf
3 cups canned or homemade chicken broth
3 cups water
salt and pepper to taste
1/2 cup half and half
1/2 cup sour cream
2 tsp. dill weed, fresh or dried
2 Tbs. fresh, finely chopped parsley or dill weed

1) Heat butter in a heavy bottomed soup pot. Sauté zucchini, onion, and garlic, stirring often, until vegetables begin to soften.

2) Add thyme, bay, broth, and water. Salt lightly if broth is unsalted. Simmer 15-20 minutes or until vegetables are tender but still bright green.

3) Remove bay leaf. Pour soup through strainer set over a bowl to separate vegetables from broth. Puree vegetables in food processor until smooth. Combine vegetables with broth and return to soup pot.

4) Whisk in half and half, sour cream, and dill. Rewarm gently, if necessary. Adjust salt and pepper. Garnish individual bowls with chopped parsley or dill.

Serves 6-8

Cauliflower Caraway Soup

4 Tbs. unsalted butter
3 cups cauliflower, sliced thin, about 1 pound
1 cup small cauliflower flowerets for garnish
1 cup chopped onion
2 tsp. caraway seed, chopped fine or ground in
  spice grinder or mortar and pestle.
1 1/2 cups canned or homemade chicken broth
2 cups water
salt and pepper to taste
2 tsp. fresh lemon juice
1 Tbs. butter
2 fresh plum tomatoes, peeled, seeded, and diced
1 Tbs. fresh, minced parsley

1) Melt butter in heavy bottomed soup pot. Add onions and sauté, stirring often, until they begin to soften.

2) Add cauliflower, excluding the 1 cup reserved for garnish, caraway seed, broth and water. Salt lightly only if broth is unsalted. Bring to a simmer and cook 25 minutes or until cauliflower is soft.

3) Pour soup through strainer set over a bowl to separate vegetables from broth. Puree cauliflower in food processor until smooth. Return to soup pot along with reserved broth. Whisk in lemon juice and add additional salt, if needed, and pepper.

4) Heat remaining 1 Tbs. butter in a small sauté pan and add the tomatoes. Cook for 2 or 3 minutes. Add salt and pepper.

5) Blanch the reserved cauliflower flowerets in boiling water for 2 or 3 minutes. Drain and quickly refresh in cold water.

6) Rewarm soup if needed. Divide among warmed soup bowls and garnish each with 3 or 4 flowerets, 1 Tbs. of tomato pieces and a sprinkle of chopped, fresh parsley.

Serves 4-6

Chilled Cucumber Soup with Shrimp

3 large cucumbers, approximately 3 pounds
1 cup coarsely chopped onion
2 tsp. fresh, minced garlic
1/2 cup white wine
1 cup chicken broth, canned or homemade
1 cup water
3/4 cup sour cream
1/2 cup heavy cream
1 tsp. fresh dill weed, minced fine
salt and pepper to taste
1/4 cup fresh, minced parsley
2 cups small, tender shrimp, approximately 1/2 pound
1/2 gallon lightly salted water
6-8 fresh dill sprigs, for garnish

1) Peel the cucumbers with a vegetable peeler and halve them length-wise. Scoop out the seeds and discard. Chop cucumbers roughly and puree in a food processor, along with onions and garlic.

2) Pour puree into a heavy bottomed soup pot with white wine, broth, and water. Bring to a simmer and cook 20-25 minutes. Remove from heat and allow to cool.

3) Stir in sour cream, cream, dill weed, salt and pepper, and parsley. Chill thoroughly.

4) Bring salted water to a boil. Add shrimp and cook 3 or 4 minutes or until shrimp are pink throughout. Drain off water, allow shrimp to cool and peel and devein. Chill shrimp thoroughly.

5) To serve, spoon approximately 4 to 6 ounces soup into a clear glass goblet. Add 5 or 6 shrimp to each and garnish with sprig of fresh dill.

Serves 6-8

Creamy Spinach Soup with Lemon

3 Tbs. butter
1 cup chopped onion
2 cups potatoes, peeled and chopped
2 tsp. fresh, minced garlic
3 10-ounce packages frozen leaf spinach
1/2 tsp. dried thyme leaves
1 bay leaf
3 cups canned or homemade chicken broth
3 cups water
salt and pepper to taste
1 cup half and half
1/3 cup sour cream
2 Tbs. fresh lemon juice
2 lemons, sliced very thin

1) Heat butter in heavy bottomed soup pot. Add onions, potatoes, and garlic and cook, stirring often, until onions begin to soften.

2) Add spinach, thyme, bay, broth, and water. Salt lightly if broth is unsalted. Simmer for 30 minutes or until potatoes are thoroughly soft.

3) Remove bay leaf. Pour mixture through a strainer set over a deep bowl to separate the vegetables from the broth. Puree the vegetables until smooth and return to soup pot along with broth.

4) Whisk in half and half, sour cream and lemon juice and adjust salt and pepper to taste. Rewarm if necessary. Garnish individual bowls with lemon slices.

Serves 4-6

Chilled Fresh Tomato Soup

4 Tbs. butter
6 cups tomatoes, preferably homegrown,
  cored and chopped coarsely
1 cup chopped onion
1 cup chopped red bell pepper
1 Tbs. fresh, chopped garlic
4 cups canned or homemade chicken broth
2 cups water
1 tsp. dried basil leaves
1 bay leaf
salt and pepper to taste
1 cup heavy cream
1/2 cup chopped, fresh cilantro

1) Heat butter in a heavy bottomed soup pot. Sauté tomatoes, onions, red bell peppers, and garlic until onions are tender.

2) Add the chicken broth, water, basil, and bay leaf. If the broth is unsalted, salt lightly. Simmer until the tomatoes are completely broken down.

3) Remove bay leaf. Pour soup through a strainer set over a bowl. Puree vegetables in food processor until smooth. Combine pureed vegetables and broth. Strain again to remove any skin and seeds.

4) Stir in cream and cilantro. Add salt, if necessary, and pepper.

5) Allow to cool and chill thoroughly before serving.

Serves 6 to 8

Gazpacho

1/2 cup green bell pepper, coarsely chopped
3/4 cup red bell pepper, coarsely chopped
3/4 cup yellow bell pepper, coarsely chopped
1 cup cucumber, peeled, seeded, and coarsely chopped
1/2 cup chopped onion
1/2 cup yellow squash, coarsely chopped
3/4 cup zucchini, coarsely chopped
1/2 cup fresh tomato, peeled, seeded, and chopped
2 cups V-8 juice
1/2 cup canned or homemade chicken broth or water
2 Tbs. fresh, minced garlic
1/2 cup finely chopped, fresh parsley
1/4 cup finely chopped, fresh cilantro
1 tsp. ground cumin
3 dashes Tabasco sauce
1 Tbs. fresh lemon juice
approximately 3/4 tsp. salt or to taste
black pepper to taste
2 Tbs. virgin olive oil
1/2 cup sour cream for garnish

1) Puree all vegetables, in batches, in food processor or blender, adding V-8 juice, as needed, to completely liquify.

2) Combine pureed vegetables, remaining V-8 juice, broth or water, all of the seasonings, and the olive oil. Blend thoroughly.

3) Chill thoroughly before serving, and garnish with sour cream.

Serves 4

Potato and Kale Soup with Fresh Tomatoes

2 Tbs. olive oil
4 cups red potatoes, peeled and chopped
1 cup onion, diced
1 Tbs. minced, fresh garlic
4 cups canned or homemade chicken broth
2 cups water
2 bay leaves
1 tsp. dried thyme leaves
3 cups fresh kale, about 1/2 pound, stemmed, rinsed,
  chopped and firmly packed into measuring cup
1 cup half and half
salt and pepper to taste
2 tsp. fresh lemon juice
1 Tbs. butter
2 fresh tomatoes, peeled, seeded, and chopped

1) Heat olive oil and sauté potatoes, onions, and garlic for 5-6 minutes, stirring often, until onions begin to soften.

2) Add broth, water, bay, thyme, and a pinch of salt, if broth is unsalted. Simmer until potatoes are soft. Remove bay leaf and discard.

3) Stir in kale and cook 2-3 minutes until kale is wilted, tender and bright green.

4) Pour mixture through strainer set over a bowl, separating broth from vegetables. Puree vegetables in food processor until potatoes are smooth and kale is ground into tiny bits. Return to soup pot along with broth.

5) Stir in half and half, lemon juice, and pepper and adjust salt, if necessary. Rewarm thoroughly.

6) Heat 1 Tbs. butter in small sauté pan. Add chopped tomatoes and quickly sauté. Salt lightly.

7) Ladle soup into individual bowls and spoon 1 Tbs. tomatoes in the center of each.

Serves 4-6

Cauliflower Soup with Dill,
Cheddar Cheese and Sour Cream

2 Tbs. clarified butter
1 1/2 cups onions, diced
2 cups carrots, peeled and diced
2 cups potatoes, peeled and diced
4 cups cauliflower, trimmed into flowerets and sliced
4 cups canned or homemade chicken broth
4 cups water
1 bay leaf
1 tsp. dried thyme leaves
1/2 tsp. caraway seed
1 Tbs. fresh, minced garlic
salt and pepper to taste
1/2 cup sour cream
1/2 cup half and half
1 Tbs. minced, fresh or dried dill weed
4 ounces sharp cheddar cheese, grated
1 cup Homemade Buttered Croutons, see page 181
1/2 cup scallions, cut into small rounds

1) Heat butter in a heavy bottomed soup pot. Add onions, carrots, potatoes, and cauliflower and sauté, stirring often, until the onions begin to soften.

2) Add broth, water, bay, thyme, caraway, and garlic. Salt lightly, if broth is unsalted. Bring to a simmer and cook 25-30 minutes or until potatoes are soft.

3) Remove bay leaf and discard. Remove 2/3 of the vegetables from the soup pot with a slotted spoon and puree in a food processor until smooth.

4) Return puree to soup pot and blend into broth and remaining vegetables. Mixture will thicken slightly.

5) Reheat gently and whisk in sour cream, half and half, dill weed and cheddar cheese. Adjust salt and add pepper to taste. Remove from heat, cover, and allow to sit 5 minutes. When cheese has melted into strands, serve in warm soup bowls garnished with Homemade Buttered Croutons and sliced scallions.

Serves 6-8

Mushroom Bisque

4 Tbs. butter
6 cups sliced mushrooms
2 cups potatoes, peeled and coarsely chopped
1 cup chopped onion
1 tsp. minced, fresh garlic
4 cups canned or homemade chicken broth
4 cups water
1 tsp. dried thyme leaves
1 bay leaf
salt and pepper to taste
1 cup half and half
1 cup Homemade Buttered Croutons, see page 181

1) Heat butter in a heavy bottomed soup pot. Sauté mushrooms, potatoes, onions, and garlic until mushrooms and onions are tender.

2) Stir in chicken broth, water, thyme, and bay leaf. Salt lightly, if broth is unsalted. Simmer for about twenty minutes or until potatoes are completely soft.

3) Remove bay leaf. Pour soup through a strainer, set over a bowl to separate vegetables from broth. Puree vegetables in food processor until smooth. Combine vegetables with broth and return to soup pot.

4) Warm gently and stir in half and half. Stir in additional salt, if necessary, and pepper. Garnish with Homemade Buttered Croutons.

Serves 6 to 8

Onion Soup with
Homemade Buttered Croutons

2 Tbs. butter
7 cups firm yellow onion, halved and sliced thin
2 Tbs. fresh, minced shallots
2 Tbs. fresh, minced garlic
4 cups canned or homemade chicken broth
4 cups water
1/4 tsp. dried thyme leaves
1 bay leaf
dash nutmeg
dash dry mustard
salt and pepper to taste
1/4 tsp. sugar
1 cup half and half
2 cups Homemade Buttered Croutons, see page 181
2 scallions or several chives sliced into thin rounds

1) Heat 2 Tbs. butter in a heavy bottomed soup pot. Add onions, shallots, and garlic and cook over medium heat until onions are soft.

2) Add broth, water, thyme, bay, nutmeg, and mustard. Salt lightly, if broth is unsalted. Cook at a low simmer for about 60 minutes or until onions are totally soft.

3) Remove bay leaf and pour mixture through a strainer set over a bowl to separate vegetables from broth. Puree cooked onions in a food processor, adding a little broth to help them liquify.

4) Return puree to soup pot along with broth. Mixture should be lightly thickened. Correct salt, add a dash of fresh black pepper and sugar. Stir in half and half and rewarm soup gently. Garnish individual bowls with Homemade Buttered Croutons and scallion rings.

Serves 6-8

Chilled Carrot and Orange Soup

This is one of my personal favorites. Thanks go out to Andy Wilkerson for sharing the recipe with us.

4 Tbs. unsalted butter
1 cup fresh shallots, finely minced
1/2 cup onions, chopped
3 cups carrots, peeled and chopped
2 cups canned or homemade chicken broth
2 1/2 cups water
1 cup freshly squeezed orange juice
1 1/2 tsp. grated orange rind
salt and white pepper
1/2 cup sour cream
2 Tbs. fresh, snipped chives

1) Heat butter in heavy bottomed soup pot. Add shallots and onions, and sauté until tender over low heat.

2) Add the carrots, broth, and water. Salt lightly, if broth is unsalted. Increase heat and simmer 20-25 minutes or until carrots are soft.

3) Pour soup through strainer set over a bowl to separate vegetables from broth. Puree vegetables in a food processor until smooth and return puree to broth. Stir until smooth and slightly thickened.

4) Stir in orange juice and rind. Adjust salt, if needed, and add a dash of fine ground white pepper. Chill thoroughly.

5) Garnish individual bowls with a swirl of sour cream and fresh snipped chives.

Serves 4-6

Canadian Cheddar Cheese Soup

4 Tbs. butter
1 cup diced onion
3 cups carrots, peeled and chopped into
  thin half-moons
3 cups potatoes, peeled and chopped into
  1/2 inch cubes
1 bay leaf
1 tsp. dried thyme leaves
4 cups canned or homemade chicken broth
4 cups water
salt and pepper to taste
4 Tbs. butter
1/2 cup flour
2 cups grated sharp Canadian cheddar cheese
1 cup half and half
2 Tbs. chopped fresh parsley

1) Heat butter in heavy bottomed soup pot. Sauté onions, carrots, and potatoes until onions are soft.

2) Add bay leaf, thyme, chicken broth, and water. Salt lightly, if broth is unsalted. Simmer until potatoes are completely soft.

3) In a separate pan, melt 4 Tbs. butter. Whisk in flour. Cook for 3 minutes, whisking constantly.

4) Whisk one cup of hot soup broth into flour paste. Return all this to the soup pot. Simmer, stirring until thickened and well blended.

5) Remove from heat. Whisk in cheddar cheese, half and half and parsley. Stir in additional salt, if necessary, and pepper. Allow to sit until cheese has melted into strands. Remove bay leaf before serving.

Serves 6-8

Carrot, Tomato, and Green Chili Soup

2 Tbs. butter
1 cup diced onion
3 cups coarsely chopped carrots
3 cups canned or homemade chicken broth
3 cups water
1 bay leaf
1 tsp. dried thyme leaves
1 tsp. dried oregano leaves
2 tsp. ground cumin
2 tsp. fresh, minced garlic
2 dashes crushed red pepper flakes, or
  more to taste
salt and pepper to taste
2 cups canned crushed red tomatoes
  in puree
2 Tbs. canned chopped green chilies
1/2 cup heavy cream
1 tsp. molasses

1) Heat butter in a heavy bottomed soup pot. Sauté onions and carrots for 5 to 10 minutes or until vegetables begin to soften.

2) Add chicken broth, water, bay leaf, thyme, oregano, cumin, garlic, and red pepper flakes. Salt lightly, if broth is unsalted. Simmer for about 30 minutes or until vegetables are completely soft.

3) Remove bay leaf. Pour soup through a strainer set over a bowl to separate vegetables from broth. Puree vegetables in food processor until smooth, adding a little broth to the puree to help vegetables liquefy. Return puree and all broth to the soup pot. Stir gently until blended.

4) Stir in tomatoes, chilies, cream, molasses, salt, if necessary, and pepper. Heat thoroughly.

Serves 6-8

Curried Winter Squash Soup

This recipe is a variation on a curried pumpkin soup that was taught to me by my good friend, John Kalmer.

6 Tbs. butter
2 medium acorn squash, peeled, seeded,
  and diced
3 cups canned or homemade chicken broth
3 cups water
1/2 tsp. curry powder
1/2 tsp. dried oregano leaves
salt and pepper
2 cups sliced, fresh mushrooms
1/2 cup minced onion
1/2 cup fresh cabbage, chopped into
  small pieces
1/4 cup half and half

1) In a heavy bottomed soup pot melt 2 Tbs. butter, add the squash and, tossing frequently, cook over medium heat until it begins to brown.

2) Add broth, water, curry, and oregano. Salt lightly, if broth is unsalted. Bring to a simmer and cook about 20 minutes or until squash is totally soft. Remove squash from broth with a slotted spoon and put into a food processor fitted with a steel blade. Puree until smooth, adding a cup of broth while machine is running to help squash liquify. Return puree to broth and set aside.

3) Heat 2 Tbs. butter in a large sauté pan and add mushrooms. Cook quickly until soft and beginning to brown, then add to the squash soup. Return sauté pan to the heat, melt another 2 Tbs. butter and add onions and cabbage. Cook over medium heat until softened, then add to the squash soup.

4) Bring soup to a low simmer and cook all together for 5 or 6 minutes. Correct salt and add a pinch of black pepper. Stir in half and half and serve.

Serves 6-8

Navy Bean Soup with Vegetables

1 cup small white navy beans, completely
* covered in water and soaked overnight*
4 cups canned or homemade chicken broth
4 cups water
2 bay leaves
1 Tbs. fresh, minced garlic
1 tsp. dried oregano leaves
1 tsp. dried thyme leaves
2 Tbs. olive oil
1 1/2 cups onion, diced
1 1/2 cups carrots, peeled and diced
1 cup zucchini, quartered lengthwise and sliced
1 1/2 cups crushed tomatoes in puree
2 Tbs. fresh, minced parsley
Up to 3 cups additional water
salt and pepper to taste

1) Drain soaking water from beans, rinse thoroughly, and put in heavy bottomed soup pot with broth and water. Bring to a boil and skim off foam that forms on top. Lower heat to a gentle simmer and add bay leaves, garlic, oregano, and thyme. Cook until beans are thoroughly soft but not mushy, adding additional water if necessary during the cooking process.

2) Heat olive oil in large sauté pan. Add onions, carrots and zucchini, and cook quickly until vegetables are tender.

3) Add vegetables to cooked beans, along with crushed tomatoes. Simmer 20-25 minutes more, adding water, salt, if necessary, pepper and parsley.

Serves 6-8

Split Pea Soup with Basil and Garlic

2 cups dried green split peas, about 1 pound
4 cups canned or homemade chicken broth
6 cups water
1 tsp. fresh, minced garlic
2 bay leaves
1/2 tsp. dried thyme leaves
2 tsp. dried basil leaves
2 Tbs. olive oil
1 cup onion, diced
3/4 cup carrot, peeled and cut into 1 inch
  long matchsticks
3/4 cup parsnips, peeled and cut into 1 inch
  long matchsticks
2 Tbs. minced, fresh parsley
salt to taste
fresh cracked black pepper

1) In a heavy bottomed soup pot, combine peas, broth and water. Bring to a boil and skim off the foam that forms on top. Lower heat to a simmer and add garlic, bay leaves, thyme and basil. Salt lightly if broth is unsalted. Cook 50-60 minutes, stirring often, until peas are soft and falling apart.

2) Remove bay leaf and discard. In batches, transfer pea mixture to the bowl of a food processor and puree until smooth. Return to soup pot and set aside.

3) Heat olive oil in large sauté pan. Add onions, carrots, and parsnips and, tossing frequently, cook over low heat until vegetables are tender. Stir vegetables into pureed peas and rewarm gently. Correct salt and stir in parsley and pepper.

Serves 6-8

Elizabeth's Vegetable Soup

Here it is, the wonderful soup I was raised on. All you need to go with it is hot cornbread muffins.

2 cups canned or homemade chicken broth
3 Tbs. vegetable oil, only if broth is fat free
2 medium potatoes, about 2 cups, peeled
* and chopped*
1 medium onion, about 1 1/4 cup, diced
2 carrots, about 2 cups, sliced thin
4 ears fresh corn, cut from cob, about 1 1/2 cups
1 cup fresh or frozen lima beans
2 cups cabbage, chopped
1 8-ounce can tomatoe sauce
1 quart home canned or fresh chopped
* tomatoes*
1 1/2 tsp. sugar
salt and pepper to taste
1/2 cup sliced okra, optional

1) Combine all ingredients in a heavy bottomed soup pot and simmer for about 1 1/2 hours. Add enough water during cooking to make about 3 quarts finished soup. Correct salt and pepper.

Serves 6-8

Crab and Corn Chowder

1/4 pound bacon, chopped fine
1 cup onion, diced
1/2 cup green bell pepper, diced
1/2 cup red bell pepper, diced
2 cups potatoes, peeled and diced
2 cups fresh white or yellow corn niblets, cut from cob
1 tsp. dried thyme leaves
1 tsp. fresh, minced garlic
2 bay leaves
4 cups bottled clam juice or homemade fish stock
4 cups water
salt and pepper to taste
4 Tbs. butter
1/2 cup flour
1 pound crab meat from Atlantic blue crab, either lump
  or claw, all shell and cartilage removed
1/2 cup half and half
1/2 cup fresh, chopped parsley

1) Place bacon in heavy bottomed soup pot and sauté over medium heat, stirring frequently, until browned and crispy. Remove bacon bits from fat with a slotted spoon and set aside. Pour off excess bacon fat leaving approximately 2 Tbs. in bottom of soup pot. Discard excess or retain for other use.

2) Add onions, peppers, potatoes, and corn and sauté, stirring often, until onions are soft.

3) Add thyme, garlic, bay leaves, bacon bits, clam juice or stock, and water. Salt lightly if broth is unsalted. Simmer until potatoes are soft.

4) In separate sauce pan, heat 4 Tbs. butter until bubbling and whisk in 1/2 cup flour. Cook 3-4 minutes, whisking constantly. Do not brown.

5) Pour 2 cups hot soup broth into flour paste, whisking until smooth. Return to soup pot, stirring until well blended and slightly thickened.

6) With soup at a low simmer, stir in crabmeat, half and half, and chopped parsley. Correct salt, if necessary, and add fresh cracked black pepper. Warm thoroughly and serve.

Serves 6-8

Florentine Fish Soup

2 Tbs. butter
1 cup diced onion
2 cups diced carrots
2 cups diced potatoes, peeled
1 tsp. fresh, minced garlic
1 tsp. dried thyme leaves
1/2 tsp. fennel seed
2 bay leaves
3/4 cup dry white wine
4 cups bottled clam juice or fine quality
* homemade fish stock*
4 cups water
salt and pepper to taste
4 Tbs. butter
1/2 cup flour
1 pound white, meaty game fish such as
* dolphin, snapper, cobia, or red drum,*
* skinned, boned, and cut into 1 inch pieces*
1/2 pound spinach, rinsed well, stemmed, and
* cut into coarse shred or 1 10-ounce package*
* frozen leaf spinach, thawed, drained, and*
* chopped*
1/2 cup half and half
1/4 cup fresh, chopped parsley

1) Melt 2 Tbs. butter in heavy bottomed soup pot and add onions, carrots, potatoes, and garlic. Cook until onions are beginning to soften, stirring occasionally. Do not allow to brown.

2) Add thyme, fennel, bay leaves, and wine. Over medium heat, allow wine to reduce by half.

3) Add clam juice or fish stock and water. Salt lightly if broth is unsalted. Simmer 20-25 minutes or until potatoes are soft.

4) In separate saucepan, heat 4 Tbs. butter and when bubbling, whisk in

1/2 cup flour. Cook 3-4 minutes whisking constantly, over low heat. Do not allow to brown.

5) Gradually pour 2 cups hot soup broth into flour paste, whisking until smooth. Return all to soup pot, stirring until well blended and slightly thickened.

6) With soup at a simmer, stir in fish chunks and spinach and cook gently 3-4 minutes until fish is cooked through and spinach is wilted. Stir in half and half and parsley. Stir in additional salt, if necessary, and fresh cracked black pepper. Serve in warm soup bowls.

Serves 6-8

Seafood Chowder
with Vegetables and Tomatoes

3 Tbs. butter
1 1/2 cups onion, diced
1 1/2 cups carrots, peeled and diced
2 cups potatoes, peeled and diced
1 tsp. dried thyme leaves
1 tsp. dried basil leaves
2 bay leaves
4 cups bottled clam juice or homemade
  fish stock
4 cups water
1 cup dry white wine
1 1/2 cups diced tomatoes in puree
salt and pepper to taste
2 pounds total mixed seafood, any
  combination - we use crabmeat, shrimp,
  scallops and fish
1/4 cup fresh, chopped parsley

1) Melt 3 Tbs. butter in heavy bottomed soup pot and add onions, carrots, and potatoes. Cook until onions begin to soften.

2) Add thyme, basil, bay leaves, broth, water, wine, and diced tomatoes in puree. Salt lightly if broth is unsalted. Simmer until potatoes are soft. Skim off oil that comes to the top.

3) Make sure seafood is free of all bones, shell, skin, cartilage, and sandy grit.

4) With soup at a simmer, stir in seafood. Poach gently until seafood is cooked through. Stir in parsley. Correct salt, if necessary, and add fresh cracked pepper.

Serves 6-8

Chicken Stock

3 pounds chicken bones, necks, backs,
* wings, etc.*
2 cups chopped onion
1 cup chopped carrots
1 cup chopped celery
1 tsp. dried thyme leaves
1 tsp. dried rosemary leaves
2 bay leaves
6 fresh parsley sprigs
12 cups cold water

1) Combine all ingredients in a heavy bottomed stockpot and bring to a boil. Skim off foam that forms on top. Reduce heat to a simmer and cook 1 1/2-2 hours.

2) Pour mixture through a strainer set over a large pot to separate broth from solids. Press on solids to extract all broth. Discard solids, then either skim fat off top of stock and use immediately or refrigerate overnight and remove congealed fat off surface before using. Freezes well.

Yields about 7 cups

Fish Stock

4 Tbs. butter
2 cups chopped onion
1 cup chopped carrots
1/2 cup chopped celery
8 medium fish frames, including heads,
  cleaned thoroughly, all blood and gills
  removed (about 4 pounds)
1 1/2 cups dry white wine
8 cups water
1 tsp. dried thyme leaves
2 bay leaves
1 tsp. dried rosemary leaves
1/2 cup parsley sprigs with stems
1 Tbs. Champagne vinegar

1) Heat oil. Add onions, carrots, and celery. Cook over medium heat, stirring occasionally, until vegetables begin to soften.

2) Add all remaining ingredients and bring to a simmer, skimming off foam. Cover and cook for 25-30 minutes.

3) Allow to cool, then pour entire contents through fine mesh strainer set over another pot or bowl. Press on solids to extract all liquid.

4) Will store in refrigerator up to two days.

Yields about 6 cups

Vegetable Stock

2 cups chopped onion
2 cups chopped celery
2 cups chopped carrots
1 cup chopped potato
2 cups chopped zucchini squash
1 cup chopped fresh tomatoe
2 cups chopped mushrooms
1 cup sliced chard leaves
6 sprigs fresh parsley
1 tsp. dried basil leaves
1 tsp. dried thyme leaves
2 bay leaves
8 cups cold water

1) Combine all ingredients in a heavy bottomed stock pot and bring to a boil. Reduce heat to a simmer and cook for 45-50 minutes.

2) Pour mixture through a strainer set over a large pot, separating vegetables from broth. Press on vegetables to extract all liquid. Discard vegetables and use broth immediately or allow to cool, then refrigerate or freeze.

Yields about 5 cups

Salads

We live in a time when food seems to know no boundaries or seasons, and one of the advantages of this is the vast abundance of salad ingredients available to us today. Feta cheese, montrachet, and imported Roquefort, luxuries I happily take for granted, were unheard of in my mom's kitchen. No longer limited to iceberg lettuce, we enjoy an enormous variety of exotic salad greens. Greek olives, balsamic vinegar, and virgin olive oil have become staples of the contemporary kitchen and an integral part of our daily fare.

At the restaurant, we have incorporated these ingredients into salads appropriate to a variety of settings. These recipes, accumulated over the years, were developed for our regular menu offerings and for the parties and receptions we cater throughout the year. In response to the growing concern about the safety of raw eggs, we recently reworked all of our dressing recipes to eliminate their use. Our best efforts culminated in the creation of an eggless Caesar Salad, which has become the house favorite.

Back Porch House Salad with Eggless Caesar Dressing

1/2 head romaine lettuce, rinsed, patted dry, and
  torn into small pieces.
1/2 head red leaf lettuce, rinsed, patted dry, and
  torn into small pieces.
1/2 cup red seedless grapes, halved
2 Tbs. grated parmesan cheese
3/4 cup Homemade Buttered Croutons, see page 181

1) Combine all ingredients in a large salad bowl and toss with approximately 1/2 cup Eggless Caesar Dressing.

Serves 4

Eggless Caesar Dressing
1 2-ounce can anchovies in oil
1 1/2 Tbs. fresh, minced garlic
1/4 cup Dijon mustard
1 1/2 Tbs. fresh cracked black pepper
2 Tbs. dried oregano leaves
1/2 tsp. salt
3/8 cup red wine vinegar
2 cups olive oil

1) In food processor, puree anchovies with their oil to form a smooth paste.

2) Add garlic, mustard, pepper, oregano, and salt. Process until blended.

3) With the processor running, add the vinegar slowly in a thin stream.

4) With the processor still running, add the oil slowly in a thin stream. Process until thoroughly blended. Dressing should be thick and creamy.

Yields 3 cups

Red Leaf and Spinach Salad
with Citrus Sections and Toasted Walnuts

1/2 head red leaf lettuce, rinsed, patted dry, and
* torn into small pieces*
1/4 pound fresh young spinach leaves, stemmed,
* rinsed, and patted dry*
2 navel oranges or 1 pink grapefruit, sections
* removed from connective tissue and seeds*
* removed, see page 187 for this procedure*
1/4 cup toasted walnuts
1/4 cup scallion tops, sliced into tiny rings

1) Combine all ingredients in a large salad bowl and toss with approximately 1/2 cup Walnut Vinaigrette.

Serves 4

Walnut Vinaigrette
1 tsp. minced, fresh shallots
1 tsp. minced, fresh garlic
1 tsp. salt
1 tsp. fresh cracked black pepper
1 Tbs. Dijon mustard
3 Tbs. apple cider vinegar
1 Tbs. fresh lemon juice
1/2 cup virgin olive oil
1/2 cup walnut oil

1) Put shallots, garlic, salt, pepper, mustard, vinegar, and lemon juice into a glass pint jar and shake vigorously.

2) Add both oils and shake vigorously before each use. Dressing will separate after sitting.

Yields about 2 cups

Bitter Greens and Avocado with
Lemon Dill Vinaigrette

1 large head Bibb lettuce, rinsed, patted dry, and torn
  into small pieces
1/4 pound chicory, arugula and / or radicchio, rinsed,
  patted dry, and torn into small pieces
1 perfectly ripe avocado, peeled and sliced
2 thin slices red onion, broken into rings
12 Nicoise or Greek olives
12-16 Herbed Chevre Croutons, see page 180

1) Combine all ingredients, except croutons, in large salad bowl and toss with about 1/2 cup Lemon Dill Vinaigrette.

2) Pass plate of Herbed Chevre Croutons separately.

Serves 4

Debbie's Lemon Dill Vinaigrette
2 Tbs. Dijon mustard
1 tsp. fresh, minced garlic
1 1/2 tsp. dried dill weed
1 tsp. salt
1/2 tsp. fresh ground black pepper
2 Tbs. fresh, minced parsley
2 Tbs. red wine vinegar
2 Tbs. fresh lemon juice
3/4 cup vegetable oil
3/4 cup olive oil

1) Combine mustard, garlic, dill, salt, pepper, and parsley in a medium mixing bowl and whisk thoroughly with a small balloon whisk.

2) Add vinegar and lemon juice and whisk again. Add vegetable oil and olive oil in a thin, steady stream, whisking constantly until dressing is thick and emulsified.

3) Store dressing in a 2 cup capacity glass jar and shake vigorously before using.

Makes 2 cups

Roquefort Waldorf Salad on Mixed Greens

1 cup Granny Smith apples, cored, sliced, and
  cut into 1/2 inch pieces
1 cup Red Delicious apples, cored, sliced, and
  cut into 1/2 inch pieces
3/4 cup chopped pecans, toasted in oven to a
  golden brown
1/2 cup minced celery
1/4 cup scallions, sliced into thin rings
1 Tbs. fresh, minced parsley
sweet, young lettuce leaves, mixed, any kind,
  enough for 4 healthy servings
8 spears Belgian endive, sliced crosswise

1) In a medium mixing bowl, combine apples, pecans, celery, scallions, and parsley with about 1/2 cup Roquefort Vinaigrette. Use a spoon to scoop out cheese chunks that settle to the bottom of the dressing and add cheese to the salad. Toss lightly, add additional salt and pepper to taste, and set aside.

2) In a large decorative salad bowl, toss mixed lettuce leaves and endive with about 1/2 cup Roquefort Vinaigrette. Mound apple salad in the center of dressed greens and serve.

Serves 4

Roquefort Vinaigrette
4 ounces Roquefort or blue cheese
1 tsp. minced, fresh garlic
1 tsp. coarse ground black pepper
1/2 tsp. dried tarragon leaves
1/2 tsp. dried basil leaves
1/2 tsp. salt
3 Tbs. red wine vinegar
1 cup olive oil

1) Crumble cheese into a glass pint jar. Add all remaining ingredients. Shake vigorously before using.

Yields about 2 cups

Mixed Greens with Balsamic Vinaigrette

1/2 head red leaf lettuce, rinsed, patted dry, and
  torn into small pieces
1/2 head Bibb or Boston lettuce, rinsed, patted
  dry, and torn into small pieces
1/4 cup red bell pepper, cut into 1 inch long
  matchsticks
1/4 cup yellow bell pepper, cut into 1 inch long
  matchsticks
4 ounces Herbed Chevre, crumbled, see page 180
1 cup Homemade Buttered Croutons, see page 181

1) Combine all ingredients in a large salad bowl and toss with about 1/2 cup Balsamic Vinaigrette.

Serves 4

Balsamic Vinaigrette
1/3 cup red wine vinegar or Andy's Herbed
  Champagne Vinegar, see page 179
2 Tbs. balsamic vinegar
1 cup virgin olive oil
1 tsp. salt
1/4 tsp. fresh cracked black pepper

1) Combine all the above ingredients in a glass pint jar and shake vigorously before each use.

Yields 1 1/2 cups

Citrus Salad with Mango

1 red or pink grapefruit
1 white grapefruit
2 navel oranges
1 lime
1 large ripe mango

1) Clean all citrus according to directions under Citrus Sections, see page 187.

2) Peel and slice mango. Add to citrus, toss, chill, and serve.

Serves 6-8

Fresh Fruit Salad
with Sour Cream Dressing

1 honeydew melon
1 cantaloupe melon
1/2 fresh pineapple
1/2 cup fresh blueberries, rinsed and
  patted dry
1 cup fresh small strawberries, rinsed
  and patted dry

1) Halve honeydew, remove seeds, and cut into small rounds with melon baller.

2) Repeat with cantaloupe

3) Peel and core fresh pineapple half and cut into half inch pieces.

4) Combine melons and pineapple, tossing gently, and place in a decorative bowl.

5) Pour blueberries and strawberries over the top of melons. Chill until ready to serve. Pass Sour Cream Dressing separately.

Serves 8

Sour Cream Dressing
1 cup sour cream
1/4 cup honey
1 Tbs. fresh lemon juice
dash of cinnamon
dash of nutmeg

1) Whisk together the above ingredients until thoroughly blended. Scoop into a decorative bowl and chill until ready to serve.

Makes about 1 cup

Debbie's Marinated Three Bean Salad

1 cup black turtle beans, soaked in water overnight
1 cup dried garbanzo beans, soaked in water overnight
1 cup red chili beans or kidney beans, soaked in
  water overnight
1 1/2 gallons water
1 1/2 tsp. salt
3 tsp. dried basil leaves
3 tsp. dried thyme leaves
3 tsp. dried oregano leaves
3 bay leaves
6 tsp. minced, fresh garlic
2/3 cup red bell pepper, diced fine
2/3 cup green bell pepper, diced fine
1/2 cup scallions, sliced into thin rounds
1/4 cup fresh, minced cilantro or parsley
1/3 cup red wine vinegar
3/4 cup virgin olive oil
1 tsp. salt
1/2 tsp. fresh ground black pepper
1 tsp. fresh, minced garlic

1) Drain soaking water off each pot of beans, rinse and return beans to their three separate pots. To each, add 1/2 gallon water, bring to a boil, then skim off foam which forms on top.

2) Add to each pot 1/2 tsp. salt, 1 tsp. basil, 1 tsp. thyme, 1 tsp. oregano, 1 bay leaf, and 2 tsp. garlic. Simmer gently until beans are soft, but not mushy. Add more water to beans during cooking, if necessary.

3) Drain cooking liquid off beans and remove bay leaves. Cool, then combine all the beans with the peppers, scallions and cilantro or parsley.

4) In a separate bowl, whisk together the vinegar, olive oil, salt, pepper, and garlic and pour over the beans, tossing thoroughly. Chill until ready to serve. Looks terrific stuffed in hollowed tomato halves.

Yields 8-10 cups

Elizabeth's Macaroni Salad

My mom's been making this macaroni salad for as long as I can remember. I've given the recipe to dozens of people over the years and, consequently, made many friends.

1/2 gallon lightly salted water
1 8-ounce package shell or elbow macaroni
1 cup sharp cheddar cheese, cut in 1/4 inch cubes
1/2 cup green onions, finely chopped
1/2 cup green Spanish olives, finely chopped
1/2 cup red bell pepper, finely chopped
1/2 cup fresh parsley, finely chopped
3/4 cup best quality mayonnaise
salt and pepper to taste

1) Bring 1/2 gallon water to a boil. Stir in macaroni and simmer until pasta is cooked. Drain and rinse with cold water. Drain again and toss pasta in a colander to relieve of any excess moisture.

2) In a large bowl, mix pasta with all remaining ingredients until evenly blended. Season with salt and pepper.

Serves 6-8

Squash Salad with Basil Lemon Dressing

1/2 gallon lightly salted water
4 small yellow squash, large bulbed
* ends only, sliced into thin rounds*
2 medium zucchini, sliced into thin
* rounds*
4 homegrown tomatoes, sliced crosswise
* into thin rounds*
8 whole basil leaves for garnish

1) Bring 1/2 gallon salted water to a boil. Add yellow squash and zucchini and cook for 2 or 3 minutes until slightly soft, still crunchy, and brightly colored. Drain and quickly plunge into bowl of ice water. After 1 minute, drain again and pat lightly with paper towels to remove excess water.

2) In a large shallow bowl, arrange vegetables in overlapping concentric circles, alternating yellow squash, zucchini, and tomatoes. Drizzle about 3/4 cup Basil Lemon Dressing over arranged vegetables and scatter whole basil leaves over the top.

Serves 8-10

Basil Lemon Dressing
2 Tbs. Champagne vinegar
1 Tbs. fresh lemon juice
1 tsp. salt
1/4 tsp. fresh ground black pepper
1 tsp. fresh, minced garlic
1 Tbs. finely chopped, fresh basil
1 cup virgin olive oil

1) In a glass pint jar, combine all ingredients and shake vigorously before using.

Yield 1 cup

Shrimp and Chicken Salad with Feta Cheese

1 gallon lightly salted water
1 pound medium shrimp, in their shells
1 pound boneless, skinless, chicken breasts, fat and
* cartilage removed*
1 Tbs. salad oil
2 cups fresh broccoli flowerets, cut to a uniform size
1/2 cup red bell pepper, cut into 1 inch matchsticks
1/2 cup yellow bell pepper, cut into 1 inch matchsticks
4 ounces feta cheese, crumbled
2 Tbs. fresh, minced parsley
1 Tbs. fresh, minced chives
1/2 pound arugula, rinsed, stemmed, and patted dry
1/2 pound fresh spinach, rinsed, stemmed, and
*   patted dry*

1) Divide the gallon of water equally between 2 pots and bring to a boil.

2) In the first pot, drop shrimp, cook until pink, drain and cool. Peel and devein shrimp. Set aside.

3) In the second pot, drop broccoli flowerets, cook 1 minute, drain and refresh in ice water. Drain again and pat dry with paper towel. Set aside.

4) Heat salad oil in medium sauté pan and add chicken breasts. Brown lightly on both sides and cook thoroughly. Remove from heat and allow to cool. Slice chicken breasts crosswise into 1/2 inch wide strips.

5) Combine shrimp, broccoli, chicken, peppers, feta, parsley, and chives. Toss with approximately 1/2 cup Lemon Dressing. Set aside.

6) Combine arugula and spinach in salad bowl. Toss with approximately 1/4 cup Lemon Dressing. Divide greens equally between 4 plates. Divide shrimp and chicken equally between 4 plates, mounding on top of greens.

Serves 4

Lemon Dressing
3 Tbs. fresh lemon juice
1 tsp. dried oregano leaves
1/2 tsp. salt
1/4 tsp. fresh cracked black pepper
1/2 tsp. fresh, minced garlic
3/4 cup virgin olive oil

1) Put all ingredients in a glass pint sized jar and shake vigorously before using.

Makes about 1 cup

Fresh Blue Crab Salad

1 pound lump meat from Atlantic blue crab, all
cartilage and shell removed
1 1/2 tsp. fresh lemon juice
1/2 cup best quality mayonnaise
salt to taste

1) Combine all ingredients in a bowl and toss lightly. Serve well chilled with crackers.

Serves 4-6

Back Porch Cobia Salad

1/2 gallon lightly salted water
1 pound fresh cobia, skinned, boned, all dark
  meat removed
1/2 cup best quality mayonnaise
1 1/2 tsp. fresh lime juice
salt and pepper to taste

1) Bring 1/2 gallon water to a boil in a medium sized saucepan.

2) Cut cobia into 2 inch pieces and add to boiling water. Lower heat and gently simmer until cobia is just cooked through. Drain and allow to cool.

3) In mixing bowl, break fish into fine flakes with a fork. Add all remaining ingredients and mix well.

4) Serve immediately with crackers.

Serves 2-4

Entrees

By the time I arrive at the restaurant every morning, the local man who catches our fish is already on his boat and far from shore. Surrounded by hungry gulls and sparkling water, he works for hours hauling in blue fish, Spanish mackerel, and trout. By mid afternoon, he's at my back door, soaking wet and covered with scales. He brings along a good story to tell from the day's trip and a big, white bucket overflowing with fish.

Imaginative presentations of our abundant local seafood make up most of the Back Porch menu. Using fresh herbs, the taste of butter, and garnishes of colorful vegetables, our recipes enhance, rather than overpower, the inherent goodness of the day's catch. We use the same creative approach as we prepare savory dishes of chicken, beef, and pasta, as well as entrees developed for our vegetarian customers. So, whatever your preference, be it casserole or crabcake, easy or elaborate, this chapter brings you the best of the Back Porch.

Fillet of Fish with Basil Scallion Butter

Preheat oven to 400°   Butter a 9 x 13 baking dish

1/2 pound salted butter, room temperature
1/4 cup Dijon mustard
1/3 cup chopped, fresh basil leaves
1/4 cup chopped, fresh parsley
1/4 cup sliced scallion tops
4 medium fish fillets, 1 1/2 to 2 pounds,
  rinsed and patted dry
2 ounces melted butter
2 ounces water
1 fresh tomato, peeled, seeded, and chopped

1) Combine butter, mustard, basil, parsley, and scallions. Cream until thoroughly blended. Set aside.

2) Place fish fillets in prepared baking dish and pour plain melted butter and water over fish.

3) Place fish on middle rack in preheated oven and cook 10-15 minutes or until fish is just cooked through.

4) Remove fish onto serving platter, bathing generously with seasoned butter, allowing it to melt into fish. Sprinkle with chopped tomato.

Serves 4

Cobia Kabobs with Lime Cilantro Butter

4 cobia steaks, approximately 2 pounds,
  skinned, boned, and cut into 1-inch cubes
4 to 6 bamboo skewers, soaked in
  water overnight
1/2 cup olive oil
1 Tbs. fresh, minced garlic
1/2 pound salted butter, room temperature
1/2 cup sliced scallion tops
1/4 cup chopped, fresh cilantro
2 Tbs. fresh, lime juice
1 1/2 tsp. fresh, minced garlic
1/2 tsp. salt
1 fresh tomato, peeled, seeded, and chopped
1 bright hot, charcoal fire (optional)

1) Divide fish cubes evenly between 4-6 skewers, puncturing flesh across the grain to insure that fish holds together.

2) Combine garlic and olive oil and pour over kabobs, coating all surfaces. Cover and refrigerate 4 hours.

3) Cream butter, scallions, cilantro, lime juice, garlic, and salt, blending thoroughly. Set aside.

4) Place kabobs on rack over hot charcoal fire or in hot sauté pan. Cook throughout, turning once.

5) Remove to serving platter and bathe generously with seasoned butter, allowing it to melt into fish. Sprinkle with chopped tomato.

Serves 4-6

Fish Marinated in Garlic with
Stewed Artichoke Hearts

*4 fish fillets, rinsed and patted dry, especially
   good with larger game fish such as dolphin,
   cobia or wahoo*
1/4 cup olive oil
1 Tbs. minced, fresh garlic
3 Tbs. olive oil
*1 13.75-ounce can artichoke hearts, drained
   and sliced*
1/4 cup sun dried tomatoes, see page 185
1/4 cup canned baby pearl onions, drained
1/4 cup sliced black olives, drained
1 1/2 tsp. dried oregano leaves
2 tsp. minced, fresh garlic
1/4 cup chopped, fresh parsley

1) Combine 1/4 cup oil and 1 Tbs. garlic and rub over fish. Refrigerate, covered, for 4 hours.

2) Heat 2 Tbs. oil in sauté pan. Add artichokes, tomatoes, onions, olives, oregano, garlic, and parsley. Stew over low heat, stirring frequently, until piping hot.

3) In another skillet, filmed with remaining 1 Tbs. oil, sauté fish over medium heat until cooked through. Remove onto serving platter and serve artichokes alongside.

Serves 4

Fillets of Fish Nippon

Preheat oven to 400°   Butter a 9 x 13 baking dish

4 to 6 fish fillets, rinsed and patted dry
1/4 cup tamari or soy sauce
1/4 cup water
2 Tbs. fresh lemon juice
1 tsp. fresh, minced garlic
1 1/2 tsp. dark sesame oil
2 Tbs. butter
1 1/2 Tbs. dark sesame oil
1/2 pound mushrooms, sliced, any variety or
 a mix of varieties
4 1/2 tsp. fresh, minced garlic
1 Tbs. fresh ginger root, peeled and minced
*1/2 tsp. hot chili oil *available in Asian markets*
1/4 tsp. salt
6 scallions, green tops only, cut into 1 inch
 long pieces
2 Tbs. sliced, toasted almonds

1) Arrange fish fillets in prepared pan in a single layer.

2) Whisk together tamari, water, lemon juice, 1 tsp. garlic, and 1 1/2 tsp. sesame oil and pour over fish.

3) Bake fillets in preheated oven for 10 to 15 minutes, or until fish is just cooked through.

4) While fish is baking, heat butter and 1 1/2 Tbs. dark sesame oil in a large skillet. Add mushrooms and sauté, tossing frequently, until mushrooms are lightly browned and soft. Add garlic, ginger root, hot chili oil and salt. Cook another 3 or 4 minutes.

5) Add the scallions, remove skillet from heat and cover. Let stand 1 minute to wilt scallion tops.

6) Remove fish fillets to serving platter. Spoon mushroom mixture over fish and pour enough of the cooking liquid from the fish over the entire dish to moisten liberally. Sprinkle with toasted almonds.

Serves 4-6

Fish Rolled in Ground Nuts
with Tomato Salsa

1/3 cup blanched, toasted almonds, ground fine
1/3 cup blanched, toasted hazelnuts, ground fine
1/3 cup pecans, ground fine
1 1/2 cups dry bread crumbs, see page 181
2 Tbs. chopped, fresh parsley
2 tsp. dried oregano leaves
1 tsp. salt
1/2 tsp. coarse black pepper
1 tsp. fresh, minced garlic
1/2 tsp. dried thyme leaves
4-6 medium fish fillets, such as bluefish, Spanish
   mackerel or sea trout, rinsed and patted dry
1/4 pound butter, melted and cooled
2 Tbs. additional butter for sautéing, if needed
1 recipe Tomato Salsa, recipe follows

1) Combine the ground nuts, bread crumbs, herbs, and spices and mix well. Set aside in a wide shallow pan. (These crumbs will keep indefinitely in the freezer.)

2) Dip fish fillets in the melted butter coating entire surface of fish. Allow excess to drip off. Press fish firmly into the nut crumbs until thoroughly coated. Lay fillets on platter or cookie sheet and refrigerate, uncovered, for two hours. Refrigerate leftover butter and use later to sauté fish.

3) Melt 2 Tbs. leftover butter, discarding white, milky residue on bottom, in large skillet until bubbly hot. Add fish fillets and cook over medium heat, turning once, until nicely browned. If necessary, cook in two batches, wiping pan and replenishing butter in between. Remove to serving platter and top with Tomato Salsa.

Serves 4-6

Tomato Salsa

1 1/2 cup chopped onion
3 Tbs. fresh, minced garlic
2 4-ounce cans chopped green chilies
1 tsp. crushed red pepper flakes
1/4 tsp. cayenne pepper
8 dashes Tabasco sauce
2 tsp. ground cumin
1 1/2 tsp. salt
1/4 tsp. sugar
1 tsp. dried oregano leaves
1/4 cup fresh, chopped parsley
1/4 cup fresh, chopped cilantro
1 Tbs. fresh lime juice
2 tsp. fresh lemon juice
1 28-ounce can crushed tomatoes in puree
1 28-ounce can diced tomatoes in juice

1) In the bowl of a food processor, process onions and garlic until liquified.

2) Transfer onions and garlic to a medium sized mixing bowl and add all remaining ingredients. Stir together and refrigerate until ready to use.

Yields 6 cups

Fillet of Fish with Shrimp and Cornbread Stuffing

Preheat oven to 375°   Butter a 9 x 13 baking dish

6 medium fish fillets
salt and pepper to taste
1 Tbs. melted butter
1/4 cup water
1 recipe Shrimp and Cornbread Stuffing, recipe follows
1 recipe Brown Lemon Butter, recipe follows

1) Arrange fillets in baking dish and sprinkle lightly with salt and pepper. Pour melted butter and water into pan around fillets.

2) Place in oven, along with Shrimp and Cornbread Stuffing and bake for 20-25 minutes or until fish is just cooked through and stuffing is thoroughly hot.

3) Remove fish to a decorative platter, surround with stuffing, and drizzle generously with Brown Lemon Butter.

Serves 6

Shrimp and Cornbread Stuffing

4 ounces butter
1 cup onion, diced
1 2-ounce jar pimiento, chopped
1/2 tsp. dried thyme leaves
1 tsp. fresh, minced garlic
16 medium shrimp, about 1/2 pound, peeled,
  deveined, rinsed, patted dry and cut in half
2 cups bread ends, crumbled into small pieces
2 cups cornbread, crumbled into small pieces
2 pinches salt or more to taste

1) Melt butter in large sauté pan. Add onions and cook until they begin to soften. Add pimiento, thyme, garlic, and shrimp and cook, stirring frequently, until onions are soft and shrimp are cooked through.

2) Place bread crumbs and cornbread crumbs in a 12 inch casserole dish. Pour entire sautéed mixture over crumbs, tossing thoroughly to blend. Add salt to taste. Place in preheated oven right before serving for 15-20 minutes until hot throughout

Makes about 6 cups

Brown Lemon Butter
2 cups dry white chablis
2 Tbs. fresh lemon juice
1 cup canned chicken broth
3 Tbs. tamari or soy sauce
1 1/2 Tbs. butter
3 Tbs. flour

1) Simmer Chablis in a medium saucepan until reduced to 1 cup. Add lemon juice, broth and tamari. Return to a simmer.

2) In another saucepan, melt butter. Add flour, whisking until smooth. Cook for 2 minutes, over low heat, whisking constantly.

3) Whisk hot liquid into flour mixture until sauce is smooth, slightly thickened and simmering. Keep warm until ready to serve or reheat gently before using.

Makes about 2 1/2 cups

Marinated Fish Fillets with Sweet Peppers

8 4-ounce fish fillets, rinsed and patted dry or 2
* pounds game fish such as wahoo or cobia, boned,*
* skinned, and cut into medallions 1/2 inch thick*
1/2 cup dry, white vermouth
1/4 cup fresh lemon juice
1/2 cup olive oil
4 1/2 tsp. fresh, minced garlic
2 1/2 tsp. dried basil leaves
1/2 tsp. dried tarragon leaves
1/4 cup chopped, fresh parsley
1/4 cup capers
1/4 tsp. fresh cracked black pepper
8 cherry tomatoes, halved
3/4 cup red bell pepper, cut into 1 1/2 inch strips
3/4 cup green bell pepper, cut into 1 1/2 inch strips
1 medium sized onion, shaved into thin slices and
* broken into rings*
4 Tbs. butter for sautéing fish

1) Place fish in single layer in shallow sided baking dish.

2) Combine vermouth, lemon juice, oil, garlic, basil, tarragon, parsley, capers, and black pepper. Whisk thoroughly and pour over fish. Add vegetables, spreading evenly over fish. Cover and refrigerate 3 hours.

3) Heat butter in sauté pan until lightly browned and smoking hot. Remove fish from marinade, raking off vegetables and marinade. Sauté fish, turning once, until nicely browned on both sides and cooked through. Salt fish liberally on both sides during the cooking process. Remove fish to serving platter and keep warm.

4) While pan is still very hot, remove vegetables from marinade with a slotted spoon and place in sauté pan. Discard remaining marinade. Cook vegetables over high heat, stirring often, until they begin to soften. Add salt and pepper to taste.

5) Spoon vegetables over fish and pour cooking juices over fish.

Serves 4

Debbie's Baked Bluefish

Preheat oven to 400°   Lightly butter a 9 x 13 baking dish

4 medium sized bluefish fillets, rinsed and
* patted dry*
salt and pepper
2 Tbs. small, best quality capers
2 Tbs. minced Spanish olives
2 Tbs. minced Calamata olives, pits removed
1/2 tsp. dried or fresh, minced oregano leaves
1/2 tsp. minced, fresh garlic
2 Tbs. extra virgin olive oil
2 Tbs. dry, white vermouth
2 Tbs. water

1) Place fillets in buttered casserole in a single layer. Sprinkle lightly with salt and pepper. Set aside.

2) Combine capers with olives, oregano, garlic, and olive oil. Spread evenly over fish fillets.

3) Mix vermouth and water together in a small bowl and pour over fish. Cover with aluminum foil and bake in preheated oven until fish is thoroughly cooked. Remove to a serving platter.

Serves 2-4

John Ivey's Fabulous Fish Cakes

If you really want to do this right, cook every thing in this recipe multiplied by two. On the first night, offer the bacon with drippings, potatoes, eggs, fish, onions, and hot sauce separately. Each person serves themselves a bit of each and mashes it all up together on their plate, making their own individual adjustments to taste as they go. Some like more bacon than others, some more onion. This is John's version of the Ocracoke Boiled Drum Dinner. Mix together all the leftovers, and you have tomorrow's fish cakes. Warning: Don't plan any strenuous activities after this meal.

> *6 ounces bacon, cut into 1/4 inch strips*
> *1/2 gallon lightly salted water*
> *1 pound red potatoes, peeled and cut*
>   *into quarters*
> *4 whole eggs in their shells*
> *1 pound red drum fillets, all bone, dark meat*
>   *and skin removed*
> *1/3 cup finely chopped onion*
> *1/4 cup scallion tops, sliced into thin rings*
> *1/2 tsp. Tabasco sauce*
> *salt and pepper to taste*
> *1 cup white cornmeal*
> *4 Tbs. vegetable oil or Crisco for frying*

1) Heat medium sized skillet and add bacon. Fry, stirring often, until bacon is browned and crispy. Leave bacon bits in their rendered fat and set aside.

2) Bring 1/2 gallon water to a boil and add potatoes. Simmer for 8-10 minutes or until partially cooked, then add eggs. Simmer another 5 minutes. When potatoes are completely soft and eggs are hard boiled, add fish and simmer until just cooked through, 3 to 4 minutes.

3) Remove fish and potatoes to a bowl with a slotted spoon. Remove eggs to a bowl of cold water and peel. Then add peeled eggs to fish and potatoes.

4) With a fork, mince fish into fine flakes, mash potatoes and eggs against the sides of the bowl and mix all together to form a coarse paste. Add bacon and all the dripping, plus onions, tabasco, salt, and pepper to taste. Blend all together thoroughly and chill 6-8 hours or overnight.

5) Divide mixture into about 1/2 cup amounts, shaping them with your hands into well formed patties. You should have about 12 fish cakes.

6) Dredge fish cakes into lightly salted white cornmeal to coat evenly, shaking off excess.

7) Heat 4 Tbs. salad oil or Crisco in large skillet. Fry fish cakes in batches, turning once to brown nicely on both sides. Remove to paper towels to drain excess oil, then to warm serving platter.

Serves 6-8

Shrimp in Tarragon and Mustard Cream

2 Tbs. butter
36 shrimp, peeled, deveined, rinsed, and
 patted dry
1 Tbs. fresh, minced shallots
1 Tbs. fresh, minced garlic
1/2 tsp. dried tarragon leaves
salt and pepper to taste
2 Tbs. brandy
2 Tbs. vermouth
1 cup heavy cream
2 Tbs. mustard
1 Tbs. fresh lemon juice
1 tsp. cornstarch
1/2 cup tomato, peeled, seeded and diced
fresh chives, cut into 3 inch lengths

1) Heat butter in a large sauté pan until bubbly. Add shrimp, toss to coat with butter, and sauté until shrimp are partially cooked through.

2) Add shallots, garlic, tarragon, salt, and pepper. Add brandy and immediately ignite with a match. Allow to burn 5-6 seconds, then cover, if necessary, to extinguish. Add vermouth and reduce cooking juices to a glaze.

3) Add cream and mustard. Stir cornstarch and lemon juice together and pour into mixture. Bring to a low simmer, stirring constantly, until thoroughly blended. Correct salt and pepper.

4) Spoon shrimp and sauce onto a serving platter and sprinkle with chopped tomatoes. Lay chives in a decorative pattern over the top.

Serves 2-4

Mediterranean Shrimp

1/2 gallon lightly salted water
1 pound fresh linguine
4 Tbs. clarified butter
32 medium shrimp, approximately 1 1/2 pounds
* peeled, deveined, rinsed, and patted dry*
4 tsp. minced, fresh garlic
4 tsp. minced, fresh shallots
2 Tbs. minced, fresh oregano
2 Tbs. minced, fresh basil
4 Tbs. capers
4 Tbs. sliced scallion tops
4 Tbs. minced, fresh parsley
4 Tbs. chopped sun dried tomatoes, see page 185
3/4 cup dry, white vermouth
3/4 canned chicken broth
4 Tbs. toasted pinenuts
4 Tbs. grated parmesan cheese
whole basil leaves for garnish

1) Bring salted water to a boil.

2) Have garlic, shallots, oregano, basil, capers, scallion tops, parsley, and tomatoes chopped, measured and mixed together in a small bowl.

3) Measure vermouth and broth, combine and set aside.

4) Drop linguine in boiling water, stirring.

5) Immediately heat 4 Tbs. butter until bubbly in large sauté pan. Add shrimp, tossing quickly to coat with butter. Add the herb, caper, and tomatoe mixture. When shrimp are slightly pink, add vermouth and broth. Bring to a simmer and cook 3 minutes or until shrimp are completely cooked through. Remove from heat.

6) When pasta is done, quickly drain and turn into large pasta platter. Pour cooked shrimp and all broth over pasta. Sprinkle with pinenuts, parmesan cheese and whole basil leaves. Serve immediately.

Serves 4-6

Shrimp, Scallops and Linguine
in Pesto Cream

1/2 gallon lightly salted water
1 pound fresh linguine
2 Tbs. clarified butter
1/2 cup minced onion
1/2 cup minced red pepper
20 medium shrimp, peeled, deveined,
* and rinsed*
20 medium scallops, small muscle removed,
* and rinsed*
1 recipe Pesto Cream
2 Tbs. grated parmesan cheese
8 fresh basil leaves for garnish

1) Bring water to a boil, add linguine, and stir once or twice.

2) Heat butter in medium sauté pan, add onion and red pepper, and cook until vegetables are soft. Add shrimp and scallops, and stir together until seafood is cooked through. Add the Pesto Cream and heat thoroughly while stirring.

3) When pasta is done, drain quickly and scoop into decorative pasta platter. Pour entire amount of shrimp, scallops, and sauce over pasta. Toss gently and top with grated cheese and basil leaves.

Serves 4-6

Pesto Cream
2 cups half and half
1 1/2 Tbs. butter
3 Tbs. flour
3/4 cup Pesto, see page 184
1/2 tsp. salt

1) Place half and half in medium saucepan and heat until a thin skin forms on the top.

2) Melt 1 1/2 Tbs. butter in another saucepan, add flour, and, whisking constantly, cook for 2 minutes.

3) Pour hot half and half into flour paste and whisk until slightly thickened, smooth, and simmering. If cream sauce retains small lumps of flour, strain and proceed.

4) Stir in pesto and salt and return sauce to a low simmer. Set aside. This sauce can be made up to two days in advance and refrigerated.

Yields 2 3/4 cups

Shrimp in Caper Butter

4 Tbs. clarified butter
32 shrimp, about 1 1/2 pound medium sized,
  peeled, deveined, rinsed, and patted dry
4 cups cooked, white rice
4 tsp. fresh, minced garlic
1 tsp. dried thyme leaves
1 2-ounce jar chopped pimiento, drained
6 Tbs. sliced scallion tops
4 Tbs. capers
4 Tbs. chopped, fresh parsley
1/2 cup dry, white vermouth
1/2 cup canned chicken broth

1) Melt butter in large sauté pan. Add shrimp and cook until shrimp are almost done.

2) Add all of the remaining ingredients at once, stir to mix well, and cook another 3 or 4 minutes until liquid is absorbed and shrimp are just cooked through.

3) Spoon onto large serving platter, arranging shrimp on top of rice.

Serves 4

Shrimp in Saffron Cream
with Linguine

1/2 tsp. saffron threads, packed into
  measuring spoon
1 Tbs. boiling water
1 Tbs. clarified butter
1 Tbs. fresh, minced shallots
2 tsp. grated lemon rind
2 tsp. dried basil leaves
1 dash cayenne
3 cups heavy cream
1/4 tsp. salt or more to taste
dash of black pepper
1 pound fresh linguine
1/2 gallon lightly salted water
2 Tbs. clarified butter
32 medium shrimp, about 1 1/2 pounds, peeled,
  deveined, rinsed, and patted dry
1/2 cup frozen, tiny green peas
2 Tbs. grated parmesan
2 Tbs. minced, fresh parsley

1) Combine saffron threads and 1 Tbs. boiling water and steep 3 minutes.

2) Heat 1 Tbs. butter, add shallots and cook until soft. Add lemon rind, basil, cayenne, saffron with steeping liquid, and cream. Bring to a low simmer and cook 25-30 minutes until cream is slightly thickened and reduced to about 2 1/2 cups. Cream should be nicely yellowed by the saffron and fully flavored. Add salt to taste and a dash of black pepper. Set aside. Saffron Cream may be made up to two days ahead of time and refrigerated.

3) Bring water to a boil and add linguine, stirring once or twice.

4) Immediately heat 2 Tbs. butter, add shrimp, and sauté until partially cooked. Add peas and cook 1 minute more. Add saffron cream and bring to a simmer. Remove from heat and keep warm.

5) When pasta is done, quickly drain, and scoop onto decorative pasta platter. Pour shrimp, peas, and saffron cream over pasta and toss gently. Sprinkle with grated parmesan cheese and chopped parsley.

Serves 4-6

Gratiné of Scallops Florentine

2 Tbs. clarified butter
1 tsp. fresh, minced garlic
2 tsp. fresh, minced shallots
2 pounds fresh scallops, rinsed, small tough
 muscle removed, and sliced crosswise, if large
1/4 tsp. dried thyme leaves
dash nutmeg
dash dry mustard
1 Tbs. fresh lemon juice
1/4 cup dry, white wine
2 cups heavy cream
1 Tbs. cornstarch
1 Tbs. water
1/4 tsp. salt or slightly more to taste
dash fresh ground black pepper
1 10-ounce package frozen leaf spinach, thawed,
 chopped, and well drained
2 Tbs. dry bread crumbs
2 Tbs. grated parmesan cheese

1) Heat butter in a large sauté pan and add garlic and shallots. Toss quickly for a minute or two, then add scallops, thyme, nutmeg and mustard. Toss again, cover, and cook scallops over medium high heat until firm throughout and tender.

2) Remove from heat and with a slotted spoon, transfer scallops to a medium mixing bowl. Set scallops aside. Add lemon juice and white wine to cooking juices in pan and return to high heat. Cook for 1 minute, then add cream and any accumulated juices settled to the bottom of scallops. Bring to a simmer. In a small measuring cup, mix cornstarch and water together, then pour into cream. Stir until slightly thickened and simmering throughout.

3) Remove sauce from heat, season with salt and pepper to taste, and pour about half the sauce over the cooked scallops. Blend thoroughly. Put the well drained spinach in a second mixing bowl and pour remaining sauce over spinach. Blend thoroughly.

4) Lightly butter a 10-inch, deep sided, casserole dish and pour creamed spinach into the bottom, pushing it against the sides to form a ring.

5) Spoon scallops into the center of spinach. Sprinkle bread crumbs and parmesan cheese over the top. Place casserole into a 400° preheated oven and bake until bubbly around the edges and crusty on the top.

Serves 4-6

Shrimp and Scallops in Puff Pastry Fish

For this recipe, you'll need either a decorative puff dough cutter, available at gourmet gadget shops, or a 5-inch saucer and a sharp knife to cut your puff pastry shells. We use a 5-inch fish shape.

1 package frozen puff pastry sheets
4 Tbs. clarified butter
20 medium shrimp, about 3/4 pound, peeled,
  deveined, rinsed, and patted dry
20 small sea scallops, about 3/4 pound, rinsed,
  and patted dry
4 Tbs. chopped, sun dried tomatoes, see page 185
4 Tbs. capers
4 Tbs. scallions, sliced into thin rings
2 Tbs. minced, fresh garlic
2 tsp. dried or fresh dill weed
4 Tbs. dry, white wine
3 Tbs. fresh lemon juice
1/4 tsp. salt or slightly more to taste
1 Tbs. fresh, minced parsley

1) Cut 4 decorative pastry shells, allowing one for each portion. If not built in to your cutter, score a 3-inch circle in the center of each shell. Bake in a 400° oven until golden and crisp. Cool. Punch down the inside of the scored circle with your finger and remove the top layers of pastry, leaving the bottom intact to create a small well. These may be baked up to six hours ahead. When you begin your sauté, pop them back into a 400° oven for 3 or 4 minutes to reheat.

2) Have all ingredients chopped, measured, and ready.

3) Melt butter in large sauté pan, add shrimp and scallops, and sauté until seafood is cooked half way through. Quickly add all remaining ingredients, bring mixture to a gentle simmer and cook another full minute. Correct salt, if necessary.

4) Place hot pastry shells on plates. Spoon shrimp, scallops and seasonings over shells dividing equally. Spoon a small amount of cooking juices over each pastry shell.

Serves 4

Scallops and Mushrooms in Puff Pastry Shells

1 package frozen puff pastry sheets
2 Tbs. clarified butter
2 cups sliced mushroom caps
1 tsp. minced garlic
1 tsp. minced shallots
1/4 tsp. dried thyme leaves
dash nutmeg
dash dry mustard
2 pounds scallops, approximately, rinsed, and
  tough side muscle removed
1 Tbs. fresh lemon juice
1/4 cup dry, white wine
2 cups heavy cream
1 Tbs. cornstarch
1 Tbs. water
1/4 tsp. salt or slightly more to taste
pinch fresh black pepper

1) Using a decorative cutter or a 5-inch saucer for a template, cut 4 pastry shells, allowing one for each portion. If not built in to your cutter, score a 3-inch circle in the center of each shell. Bake in a 400° oven until golden and crisp. Remove to a rack and cool. Punch down the inside of the scored circle with your fingers and remove the top layers of pastry, leaving the bottom intact to create a small well. These may be baked up to 6 hours ahead. When ready to serve, place the shells back into a 400° oven for 3 or 4 minutes to reheat.

2) Heat butter in a large sauté pan, add mushrooms, garlic, and shallots, and cook until mushrooms are soft. Stir in thyme, nutmeg, and mustard.

3) Add scallops and cook, covered, until scallops are firm and tender. Remove scallops and mushrooms from the pan with a slotted spoon and set aside. Add lemon juice and wine to the remaining cooking juices and simmer for 1 minute. Add cream and return to a simmer. Combine cornstarch and water in a small bowl and stir into simmering sauce until slightly thickened.

4) Season sauce with salt and pepper, then return scallops and mushrooms to sauce. Rewarm gently and divide equally over hot pastry shells. Garnish as desired.

Serves 4

Fried or Sautéed Scallops with
Homemade Tartar Sauce

Fried Scallops

1/2 cup vegetable oil or Crisco for frying
2 pounds scallops, rinsed, patted dry, and cut
  in half crosswise, if large
1 cup cracker meal
8 lemon wedges
2 Tbs. minced, fresh parsley
1 recipe Tartar Sauce, recipe follows

1) Heat vegetable oil or Crisco in a large, dry, heavy bottomed skillet. Drop a few grains of cracker meal into oil. When they float and sizzle, the oil is hot enough to proceed.

2) Toss scallops in cracker meal to coat thoroughly. Gently lift scallops out of meal and put into hot frying oil. Do not overcrowd pan. Cook in batches, if necessary. Cook for a minute allowing scallops to brown, then turn them over and cook another minute. When lightly browned all over and cooked throughout, remove from oil with slotted spoon or spatula onto a paper towel to remove excess oil. Place on serving platter, surround with lemon wedges and sprinkle with parsley. Pass Tartar Sauce separately.

Serves 4-6

Sautéed Scallops

2 Tbs. clarified butter
2 pounds fresh scallops, rinsed, patted dry,
  and cut in half crosswise, if large
1/4 tsp. salt or more to taste
1 Tbs. fresh lemon juice
2 Tbs. fresh, minced parsley
1 recipe Tartar Sauce, recipe follows

1) Melt butter until bubbly in a large sauté pan. Add scallops and cook quickly, allowing to brown lightly on both sides. Do not overcrowd pan. Cook in batches, if necessary, then return all to pan for final step.

2) Lower heat, add salt to taste, and lemon juice. Stir quickly and remove to serving platter. Sprinkle with fresh chopped parsley and pass Tartar Sauce separately.

Serves 4-6

Tartar Sauce
1 cup best quality mayonnaise
1/4 cup sweet pickle relish
1 tsp. fresh lemon juice
1 Tbs. finely minced pimiento
2 Tbs. finely minced onion
1 tsp. finely minced capers
dash paprika
dash fresh black pepper
dash dry mustard
salt to taste

1) Combine all ingredients and stir to blend thoroughly.

Makes 1 1/2 cups

Back Porch Crab Cakes with
Sweet Red Pepper Sauce

1 pound backfin lump meat from the
  Atlantic blue crab
2 Tbs. butter
2 Tbs. minced onion
2 Tbs. minced red bell pepper
3 Tbs. flour
1 cup heavy cream
1/2 cup plain white flour
4 Tbs. butter for sautéing crab cakes
1 recipe Sweet Red Pepper Sauce, recipe follows

1) Pick through crabmeat and remove all shell and cartilage. Set aside.

2) Melt 2 Tbs. butter in small saucepan. Add onions and pepper and cook until soft. Add flour, whisking to form a smooth paste, and cook another 3 minutes over low heat, stirring often.

3) Add cream and bring to a full simmer, whisking constantly, until mixture is very thick and pasty. Stir in crabmeat until thoroughly blended. Remove from heat, cool, then chill mixture thoroughly.

4) To form crab cakes, divide mixture evenly into 8 mounds weighing between 2 and 3 ounces. Roll each mound between your hands to form a ball. Flatten slightly, then dust with flour. Chill again for 1 hour before cooking.

5) Melt 4 Tbs. butter in large sauté pan until very hot. Add crab cakes and cook, turning once, until browned on both sides. Serve in a pool of Sweet Red Pepper Sauce.

Serves 2-4

Sweet Red Pepper Sauce

2 Tbs. butter
2 cups red bell pepper, coarsely chopped
2 Tbs. butter
2 tsp. fresh, minced garlic
2 tsp. fresh, minced shallots
2 Tbs. plain white flour
1 cup canned chicken broth
1/4 tsp. sugar
1/2 cup half and half
2 Tbs. green onion tops, sliced into tiny rings
salt and pepper to taste

1) Heat 2 Tbs. butter in a small sauce pan, add chopped red pepper, and cook, covered, over low heat until very soft. Stir often. Transfer entire mixture to the bowl of a food processor fitted with a metal blade and puree until very smooth. Set aside.

2) In the same saucepan, heat second 2 Tbs. butter and add garlic and shallots. Cook over low heat until softened. Add flour, whisk to form a smooth paste, and cook another 3 minutes.

3) Add chicken broth, red pepper puree and sugar. Bring to a simmer, whisking constantly. Stir in half and half, onions, and salt and pepper to taste. Rewarm gently before serving, if necessary. May be made up to 2 days in advance.

Makes about 2 cups

Lump Crab, Sun Dried Tomatoes, and Basil on Angel Hair

1/2 gallon lightly salted water
8 ounces fresh angel hair pasta
4 ounces clarified butter
1 cup diced bell pepper, equal parts red,
* yellow and green*
1/4 cup sliced scallions
1/4 cup chopped, sun dried tomatoes, see page 185
1 Tbs. fresh basil leaves, chopped or 1 tsp. dried
* basil leaves*
16 ounces lump crab meat from the Atlantic
* blue crab*
1/2 cup dry, white wine
1/2 cup canned chicken broth
2 Tbs. fresh, chopped parsley
2 Tbs. fresh, grated parmesan cheese

1) Bring 1/2 gallon water to a boil. Drop pasta into boiling water, stir and immediately begin step 2.

2) Melt butter in large sauté pan, add peppers and onions, and cook until vegetables begin to soften. Add tomatoes, basil, crab, wine, and broth. Bring mixture to a simmer and cook 2 minutes.

3) Drain pasta, when cooked, and scoop onto a large pasta platter. Spoon crab mixture and all cooking liquids over the pasta. Sprinkle top with parsley and parmesan.

Serves 4

Andy's Awesome Beef Stir Fry

1 Tbs. cornstarch
2 Tbs. soy sauce
3 Tbs. vegetable oil
1 pound lean, tender, beef chunks
1 red bell pepper, cut into 1 inch pieces
1 green bell pepper, cut into 1 inch pieces
1 medium onion cut into wedges
2 tomatoes, cored, and cut into wedges
1 tsp. sugar
1 Tbs. dry sherry
2 Tbs. water
1/2 tsp. salt

1) Combine cornstarch, soy sauce, and 1 Tbs. of the vegetable oil. Pour over meat and refrigerate for 24 hours.

2) Remove meat from marinade, reserving any leftover marinade. Sauté meat in remaining 2 Tbs. of oil until well browned. Remove to a platter and set aside.

3) Add peppers and onions to same sauté pan cooking until crisp but tender.

4) Return beef to sauté pan with all accumulated juices. Add tomatoes, sugar, sherry, water, and salt, along with any remaining marinade. Bring to a simmer, stirring until sauce is thickened. Serve with steamed white or brown rice.

Serves 4-6

Filet Mignon en Pipérade with Roquefort Butter

2 Tbs. clarified butter
4 8-ounce beef tenderloins
salt and pepper to taste
hot charcoal fire optional

1) Heat 2 Tbs. butter in heavy skillet or have hot charcoal fire ready for cooking. Add beef tenderloins, salt and pepper liberally, and cook to preferred doneness.

2) On individual plates, spoon pipérade into a small circle and place tenderloin in the center. Place a spoonful of Roquefort Butter on top of the beef. Garnish as desired.

Serves 4

Roquefort Butter
4 ounces unsalted butter, room temperature
5 ounces Roquefort cheese, room temperature

1) Cream butter and cheese together until blended. Set aside until ready to serve.

Makes about 1 cup

Pipérade
2 Tbs. olive oil
1 medium onion, shaved into thin slices and
  broken into rings
3/4 cup green bell pepper, cut into 1-inch
  long matchsticks
3/4 cup red bell pepper, cut into 1-inch
  long matchsticks
1 Tbs. fresh, minced garlic

1/2 tsp. dried basil leaves
1/4 tsp. dried tarragon leaves
1/4 tsp. salt
1/8 tsp. fresh ground black pepper
1 Tbs. fresh, chopped parsley

1) Heat olive oil in large sauté pan. Add all ingredients, except parsley, and cook over low heat until peppers are soft. Stir in parsley. Rewarm, if necessary, before serving.

Makes about 1 1/2 cups

Marinated New York Strip Steaks with Horseradish Sauce

4 10 to 12 ounce New York strip steaks
1/2 cup worchestershire sauce
1 bay leaf
1/2 tsp. dried thyme leaves
1/2 tsp. dried rosemary leaves
1/2 tsp. fresh, minced garlic
3/4 cup vegetable oil

1) Place steaks in shallow pan. Combine remaining ingredients, stir until blended, and pour over steaks. Refrigerate 6-8 hours.

2) Remove steaks from marinade and cook to preferred doneness. Serve with Horseradish Sauce on the side.

Serves 4

Horseradish Sauce
1 cup sour cream
3 Tbs. horseradish
2 tsp. worchestershire sauce
1/2 tsp. salt

1) Combine all ingredients. Stir until thoroughly blended and refrigerate until ready to use.

Makes 1 1/4 cups

Bourbon Pecan Chicken

1/4 cup Dijon mustard
1/4 cup dark brown sugar
2 Tbs. + 2 tsp. bourbon
2 Tbs. soy sauce
1 tsp. worchestershire sauce
1/2 cup finely ground pecans
1/2 cup dry bread crumbs
4 double breasts of chicken, boned,
  trimmed, and split into 8 pieces
4-6 Tbs. clarified butter
6 ounces chilled, unsalted butter, cut
  into 12 pieces
1/2 cup scallion tops, sliced into small rounds

1) Whisk together mustard, sugar, bourbon, soy, and worchestershire. Set aside.

2) Mix together pecans and bread crumbs. Press chicken breasts firmly into crumbs, coating well.

3) Heat 2 Tbs. butter in large skillet until bubbly hot. Add chicken breasts and cook until nicely browned on both sides and cooked through. If necessary, cook chicken in batches, wiping pan clean, and replenishing butter between batches.

4) In a small saucepan, bring the bourbon mixture to a low simmer watching carefully. Remove from heat and, whisking constantly, add the 6 ounces of butter, 1 piece at a time. Allow each piece of butter to melt before adding another. Do not reheat sauce.

5) Arrange chicken on plates, allowing 2 pieces per person. Pour sauce over chicken and sprinkle with sliced scallions.

Serves 4

Marinated Chicken Breasts with Honey Mustard Glaze

1/3 cup worchestershire sauce
1 small bay leaf
1/2 tsp. dried thyme leaves
1/2 tsp. dried rosemary leaves
1/2 tsp. fresh, minced garlic
1/2 cup vegetable oil
4 double breasts of chicken, boned,
  trimmed, and split into 8 pieces
2 Tbs. clarified butter

1) Put chicken breast in a shallow baking dish. Combine worchestershire, bay leaf, thyme, rosemary, garlic, and oil. Pour over chicken breasts and refrigerate 4 to 6 hours.

2) In a large skillet, heat 2 Tbs. butter until bubbly. Remove chicken from marinade, place in the hot butter and saute. Turn chicken frequently, basting both sides each time with the Honey Mustard Glaze. Cook until nicely browned and cooked through. Arrange on decorative platter.

Serves 4

Honey Mustard Glaze
3 Tbs. Dijon mustard
2 Tbs. honey
1 Tbs. sour cream

1) In a small mixing bowl, whisk together mustard, honey, and sour cream. Set aside.

Makes about 1/2 cup

Spinach and Artichoke Heart Casserole

Preheat oven to 350°

Lightly butter a deep 10-inch baking dish or casserole

2 Tbs. clarified butter
1 1/4 cup onion, diced
2 cups mushrooms, sliced
4 10-ounce packages frozen leaf spinach,
  thawed, drained, and chopped
1 pound cream cheese, room temperature
1 cup butter, melted
1 13.75-ounce can artichoke hearts, drained
  and sliced
3 Tbs. fresh lemon juice
5 Tbs. grated parmesan cheese
1 tsp. salt
1/2 tsp. freshly ground black pepper
4 slices Swiss cheese
1/4 cup dry bread crumbs
2 Tbs. additional parmesan cheese for top

1) Melt 2 Tbs. butter in a large sauté pan. Add onions and mushrooms and cook until soft. Add spinach and continue cooking until warmed throughout. Remove from heat, place in a large mixing bowl and add cream cheese, butter, artichoke hearts, lemon juice, parmesan cheese, salt, and pepper.

2) Blend thoroughly and pour into baking dish. Lay sliced Swiss cheese on top, sprinkle with bread crumbs and parmesan cheese. Bake in preheated oven for 35 minutes or until bubbly around the edges and lightly browned on top.

Serves 8-10

Spring Vegetables and Linguine with Chevre and Walnuts

1/2 gallon lightly salted water
1 pound fresh linguine
2 Tbs. clarified butter
1/2 cup red bell pepper, cut into 1 inch matchsticks
1/2 cup green bell pepper, cut into 1 inch matchsticks
1/2 cup yellow bell pepper, cut into 1 inch matchsticks
1/2 cup carrot, cut into 1 inch matchsticks
1 cup snow pea pods, trimmed
1 cup asparagus spears cut into 1 inch lengths
1 cup canned chicken broth or homemade
  vegetable broth
1 recipe Dill Shallot Butter, recipe follows
2 Tbs. scallions, green tops only, sliced
4 ounces chevre, crumbled
1/2 cup coarse walnut pieces, toasted

1) Bring salted water to a boil. Have all remaining ingredients prepared and measured. Drop linguine into boiling water and immediately proceed.

2) Heat 2 Tbs. clarified butter in sauté pan. Add peppers, carrots, peas, and asparagus and cook over medium heat, tossing frequently, until vegetables begin to soften and are bright in color.

3) Add broth and Dill Shallot Butter and bring to a simmer. Cook 2 minutes, until butter is melted and broth is slightly reduced. Remove from heat.

4) When pasta is done, quickly drain and turn into large pasta platter. Pour vegetables and all liquid over pasta. Arrange as necessary to evenly distribute vegetables and to coat pasta with broth. Sprinkle scallions, chevre and walnuts over the top of pasta and serve immediately.

Serves 4

Dill Shallot Butter

4 ounces salted butter, room temperature
1 Tbs. minced, fresh shallots
1 Tbs. dried dill weed
1 Tbs. minced, fresh parsley
1 tsp. minced, fresh garlic
1 tsp. Dijon mustard
1 dash cayenne pepper
1 Tbs. grated lemon rind

1) Cream together the above ingredients. Set aside.

Cuban Black Bean and Monterey Jack Cheese Casserole

This recipe takes 1st prize for the most requested Back Porch recipe of all time. We've received so many letters, phone calls, and newspaper inquiries about this one dish, it is truly amazing. Try it and find out what all the fuss is about.

2 cups dried black beans, picked over for
  rocks, covered completely with water,
  and soaked overnight
1/2 gallon water
1 tsp. salt
1 bay leaf
2 tsp. dried oregano leaves
2 tsp. dried thyme leaves
2 tsp. fresh, minced garlic
1 1/4 cup water
1/2 cup white rice
dash salt
2 Tbs. vegetable oil
1 1/2 cups onion, diced
1 cup green bell pepper, diced
1 cup red bell pepper, diced
2 tsp. fresh, minced garlic
1 cup dry, white wine
1 cup chicken or vegetable broth
1/4 tsp. salt or more to taste
2 dashes coarse black pepper
1/4 tsp. crushed red pepper flakes
4 tsp. ground cumin
1 cup golden raisins
1 cup blanched, slivered almonds
4 cups, about 1 pound, grated Monterey
  Jack Cheese
1/4 cup dry bread crumbs

1) Drain soaking water from beans, rinse thoroughly, and put in a heavy bottomed soup pot with 1/2 gallon water. Bring to a boil, skim off the foam that forms on top, then add salt, bay leaves, oregano, thyme, and garlic. Cook, covered, for about 2 hours or until beans are soft and the liquid is thick. Check and stir often.

2) Bring 1 1/4 cup water to a boil in a small sauce pan. Add rice and dash of salt, cover, and lower heat. Cook until rice is soft and all water is absorbed. Set aside.

3) Heat 2 Tbs. salad oil in large sauté pan. Add onions, red and green peppers, and garlic. Sauté until peppers and onions are soft.

4) When beans are done, add the cooked rice, sautéed onion and pepper mix, wine, broth, salt, black pepper, red pepper flakes, cumin, raisins and almonds. Stir well to thoroughly blend and cook over low heat for 8-10 minutes or until mixture begins to thicken. Correct salt if necessary.

5) Butter a deep 10 x 13 casserole dish and cover bottom and sides with the grated cheese, reserving 3/4 cup for the top. Fill with the bean mixture. Sprinkle reserved cheese and bread crumbs over the top.

6) Bake in a 375° oven for 30-35 minutes or until top is crusty and beans are bubbling.

Approximately 6-8 servings

Spinach and Brown Rice Casserole

Preheat oven to 350°   1 9-inch casserole dish,
                                            lightly buttered

2 cups boiling water
1/4 tsp. salt
1/2 bay leaf
1 cup short grain, organic brown rice
2 Tbs. clarified butter
1 cup diced onion
1 cup sliced mushrooms
1/2 cup minced celery
1 10-ounce package frozen leaf spinach,
* thawed, drained, and chopped*
2 tsp. fresh, minced garlic
4 whole eggs
1/2 pound ricotta cheese
1 cup grated cheddar cheese
2 Tbs. melted butter
1 tsp. soy sauce
1/4 tsp. dried thyme leaves
1/4 tsp. salt
pepper to taste
2 Tbs. toasted sunflower seeds

1) Add salt, bay leaf, and rice to boiling water. Cook, covered, over low heat for about 30 minutes or until rice is soft and all the water is absorbed. Set aside.

2) Melt 2 Tbs. butter in a sauté pan. Add onions, mushrooms, and celery, and cook, tossing frequently, until vegetables are soft. Add spinach and garlic, and cook three minutes more.

3) Combine spinach mixture with rice, eggs, ricotta, 1/2 cup cheddar cheese, melted butter, soy, thyme, salt, and pepper. Mix well.

4) Pour into prepared casserole. Top with remaining 1/2 cup cheddar cheese and sunflower seeds.

5) Bake in a 350° oven until lightly browned and slightly puffed on top.

Serves 6-8

Black Bean Chili

2 cups dried black beans, soaked in a
* generous amount of water overnight,*
* drained, and rinsed*
1/2 gallon water
3 bay leaves
1 Tbs. fresh, minced garlic
1 Tbs. dried basil leaves
1 Tbs. dried oregano leaves
1 tsp. salt
2 Tbs. olive oil
1 cup chopped onion
1 Tbs. fresh, minced garlic
1 28-ounce can whole tomatoes with juice
2 cups water
1 4-ounce can green chilies, chopped
1 Tbs. dried oregano leaves
1 Tbs. ground cumin
1/4 tsp. dried red pepper flakes
1/2 tsp. salt or more or less to taste
fresh ground black pepper
1/2 cup sour cream
1/2 cup finely sliced scallions
1 cup grated cheddar cheese

1) Combine beans and water in a heavy soup pot, bring to a boil, and skim off froth that forms on top. Lower heat to a simmer, add bay leaves, garlic, basil, oregano, and 1 tsp. salt. Cook 1 1/2 to 2 hours, until beans are soft and liquid is reduced to a thick consistency.

2) In a medium sauté pan, heat 2 Tbs. olive oil and add onions and garlic. Cook until onion is soft and beginning to brown. Add to beans.

3) Drain tomatoes, reserving juice. Chop tomatoes into 1/2 inch pieces and add to beans, along with all juice.

4) Add water, chilies, oregano, cumin, red pepper flakes, salt and pepper to taste. Cook chili at a low simmer for 30 to 45 minutes or until thick in texture and fully flavored.

5) Spoon into bowls and garnish with grated cheese, sour cream, and scallions.

Serves 4

Breads

I'm constantly amazed at the number of southern cooks I meet who don't bake yeast breads. Although they love yeast breads and want to make them, they never actually do. I believe this is because, as southerners, very few of us ever saw our mothers make yeast breads. My mom makes cornbread two or three nights a week, and it comes so naturally she doesn't even need a recipe. She starts throwing ingredients into a bowl and, presto, perfect cornbread every time. It's the same story with her biscuits. But on those nights when she serves spaghetti or lasagne, out pops the little frozen dinner rolls from the A&P.

So when it comes to baking yeast breads, I can claim to be totally self-taught. When we first opened The Back Porch, we served breakfast and operated a small bakery counter selling doughnuts, pastries, cookies, cakes and, of course, homemade bread. This lasted for two years, but became a terrible strain on the staff who operated the kitchen almost around-the-clock. We finally closed the bakery and stopped serving breakfast, but we have continued to bake fresh bread every day for our nightly dinner customers.

The only advice I can offer to those who want to learn about yeast breads is to just do it. Pick a recipe and make a different loaf every week for the next four weeks At the end of the month, you'll know more than I could ever tell you about bread baking. I read somewhere that all bread requires is time and a little warmth. Nothing else in the kitchen offers such rich rewards for so humble a price.

Debbie's Walnut Bread

1/2 cup warm water
2 Tbs. yeast
1/2 tsp. sugar
2 cups milk
4 Tbs. butter
1 Tbs. salt
1/2 cup honey
1/4 cup molasses
2 1/2 cups whole wheat flour
2 1/2 cups unbleached white flour
1 1/2 cups rye flour
1 cup wheat bran
1 cup raw wheat germ
1 cup roasted sunflower seeds
1 cup chopped walnuts

1) Dissolve yeast and sugar in warm water until yeast is bubbly.

2) Combine milk, butter, salt, honey, and molasses in saucepan and heat until just warmed.

3) In large mixing bowl, combine and blend all flours, wheat bran, wheat germ, sunflower seeds, and walnuts.

4) Combine yeast and milk mixture, then pour over dry ingredients. Stir together until dough is formed. Turn onto a floured work surface and knead 4-5 minutes or until dough is elastic and smooth.

5) Place in a lightly oiled bowl, turn once to coat the dough in oil, cover with a towel, and place in a warm draft free space.

6) When dough has doubled in bulk, punch down, re-knead several times and divide equally. Form into 2 round or oblong free form loaves and place on a lightly oiled baking sheet. Cover again with a towel and place in a draft free space. When almost doubled in size, place in a preheated 350° oven. Bake 40 to 45 minutes or until lightly browned and hollow sounding when thumped. Remove to a rack to cool completely.

Two loaves

Braided Italian Bread

2 Tbs. dry yeast
1 1/2 cups warm water
1 1/2 Tbs. sugar
3 cups unbleached white flour
1 1/2 cups milk
1 1/2 Tbs. sugar
1 1/2 Tbs. salt
1/4 cup butter
5 cups unbleached white flour

1) Dissolve yeast and sugar in warm water until yeast is bubbly. Stir in 3 cups flour until thoroughly blended to form a stiff sponge. Cover and set in a warm draft free space.

2) Combine milk, sugar, salt, and butter in a small saucepan. Warm gently over low heat until milk is room temperature, sugar and salt are dissolved, and butter is melted.

3) When sponge has doubled in bulk, punch down and work in warmed milk mixture and remaining 5 cups flour. When you have a rough, scrappy looking dough, turn it onto a lightly floured work surface and begin to knead. Dough will be soft and sticky at first. Sprinkle additional flour over dough as needed. Stop adding flour when dough ceases to stick to work surface. It will still be slightly tacky. Continue to knead an additional 8 minutes until dough is smooth and elastic. Place in lightly oiled bowl, turn once, cover with towel and set in draft free, warm space until doubled in bulk.

4) Punch down, re-knead several times and divide the dough equally into two parts. Take the first piece of dough, divide it into three equal parts and rolling the dough back and forth under your hands, form 3 snakes about 12 inches long. Join them together at one end with a firm squeeze and form a braid. Securely join second end by squeezing dough together and tucking under. Place loaf on lightly oiled tray. Repeat with second piece of dough.

5) Cover with towel, place in warm, draft free space and when almost doubled in bulk, place in a preheated 350° oven. Bake for 35-45 minutes or until golden brown and hollow sounding when thumped. Remove to a rack to cool completely.

Two loaves

Basic Whole Wheat Bread

2 Tbs. yeast
1 Tbs. sugar
1 1/2 cups warm water
4 Tbs. butter
1/2 cup honey
1 1/2 cups warm water
1 Tbs. salt
4 1/2 cups whole wheat flour
4 cups unbleached white flour
1/2 cup raw wheat germ
1/2 cup wheat bran

1) In a large mixing bowl, dissolve yeast and sugar in warm water until bubbly.

2) In a small sauce pan, combine butter, honey, the additional 1 1/2 cups water, and salt. Warm gently over low heat until butter and honey are liquified. Do not over heat. Mixture should be just warm to the touch. Add to yeast mixture.

3) In a medium mixing bowl, combine whole wheat flour, white flour, wheat germ, and bran. Blend thoroughly, then stir into liquid mixture. With a wooden spoon, stir ingredients together to form a rough, scrappy dough.

4) Turn dough onto work surface and knead 6-8 minutes or until dough becomes smooth and elastic. Place in lightly oiled bowl, turn once, cover with a towel, and place in a warm draft free space.

5) When dough has doubled in bulk, return to work surface, re-knead several times and divide in half. Roll each piece of dough into an 8 inch long loaf and place in 2 lightly greased 5x9 inch loaf pans. Cover again with a towel and place in a draft free space.

6) When almost doubled in bulk, place loaves in a preheated 400° oven and bake for 15 minutes. Reduce heat to 350° and bake for an additional 40-45 minutes. When done, remove loaves from pans, and place on rack to cool completely.

Two loaves

Dark Herb Bread

2 Tbs. yeast
1 Tbs. sugar
1/2 cup warm water
3 cups whole wheat flour
2 cups unbleached flour
1 cup rye flour
1/2 cup raw wheat germ
1/2 cup wheat bran
1/4 cup olive oil
2 cups warm water
1 Tbs. salt
1 tsp. black pepper, coarsely ground
1 tsp. fresh, minced garlic
1 tsp. dried or fresh rosemary leaves
1/4 cup fresh, chopped parsley

1) In a large mixing bowl, dissolve yeast and sugar in warm water until foamy.

2) Add all remaining ingredients and blend thoroughly to incorporate all the flour.

3) Turn dough onto well floured work surface and knead 4-6 minutes or until dough is elastic and smooth. Place dough in lightly oiled bowl, turn once, cover with a towel, and place in a warm, draft free space.

4) When dough has doubled in bulk, punch down, re-knead several times, and divide equally. Form into 2 round or oblong free form loaves and place on a lightly oiled baking sheet. Cover again with towel and place in draft free space. When almost doubled in size, place in a preheated 350° oven. Bake 40-45 minutes until lightly browned and hollow sounding when thumped. Remove to a rack to cool completely.

Two loaves

Onion and Tomato Focaccia

2 Tbs. dried sage leaves
2 Tbs. dried rosemary leaves
1 bay leaf
2 cups boiling water
2 Tbs. yeast
2 tsp. sugar
1 Tbs. olive oil
2 cups onion, diced
1 Tbs. fresh, minced garlic
1/2 cup sundried tomatoes, packed in oil, chopped
1 Tbs. fresh, minced parsley
5 1/2 cups unbleached white flour
1/4 cup whole wheat flour
1 Tbs. rosemary leaves

1) In a medium mixing bowl, combine sage, rosemary, bay, and boiling water. Allow to cool to room temperature and strain, removing and discarding herbs, and keeping flavored water.

2) Add yeast and sugar to cooled herbed water and set aside until yeast is bubbly.

3) In a large sauté pan, heat 1 Tbs. olive oil, add onions and garlic, and cook until onions are soft. Stir in tomatoes and parsley. Blend well and remove from heat. Allow to cool.

4) Add white and whole wheat flours to yeast mixture, stirring well. Stir in onion mixture and form a soft ball of dough.

5) Turn dough onto floured work surface and knead lightly. Dough will be quite soft and a bit sticky. Continue to knead 4 or 5 minutes, adding flour to work surface as needed.

6) Put dough in lightly oiled bowl, turn once, cover, and put in a warm, draft free space until doubled in bulk.

7) Punch down and cut in half. Place dough on 2, lightly oiled, 12-inch round pizza pans and press into flat discs. Set in warm spot and allow to rise until almost doubled in bulk. Sprinkle the loaves with rosemary leaves and place on the middle rack of a preheated 400° oven. Bake until golden and hollow sounding when thumped, about 30-35 minutes. Cut into wedges and serve warm.

Two loaves

Black Bread

2 Tbs. yeast
1/3 cup honey
1 cup warm water
2/3 cup molasses
3 cups warm water
3 cups unbleached flour
4 cups whole wheat flour
2 cups rye flour
2 cups wheat bran
2 cups raw wheat germ
1 cup rolled oats
1 Tbs. + 1 tsp. salt
1/2 cup sunflower seeds

1) In a large mixing bowl, dissolve yeast and honey in 1 cup warm water until yeast is bubbly.

2) Add molasses, 3 cups warm water, and all dry ingredients. Blend thoroughly to incorporate all the flour.

3) Turn onto floured work surface and knead 4-5 minutes or until dough is elastic and smooth. Place in a lightly oiled bowl, turn once, cover with a towel, and place in a warm, draft free space.

4) When dough has doubled in bulk, punch down, re-knead several times, and divide the dough equally into two parts. Form into 2 round or oblong free form loaves and place on a lightly oiled baking sheet. Cover again with a towel and place in a warm spot. When almost doubled in bulk, place in a preheated 400° oven for 15 minutes. Reduce heat to 350° and continue to bake an additional 40 minutes or until lightly browned and hollow sounding when thumped. Remove to a rack to cool completely.

Two loaves

Perfect Corn Bread Muffins

Preheat oven to 425°   Grease 2 2-inch muffin tins

1 cup white flour
1/4 cup sugar
4 tsp. baking powder
1 tsp. salt
1 cup white or yellow cornmeal
2 eggs
1 cup buttermilk
1/4 cup salad oil

1) Combine flour, sugar, baking powder, salt, and cornmeal. Blend lightly with a balloon whisk.

2) Combine eggs, buttermilk, and salad oil. Whisk lightly with a balloon whisk.

3) Pour egg mixture into dry ingredients. Fold together with a rubber spatula until just blended. Spoon batter into muffin tins and bake until golden around edges and lightly browned on tops.

Yields 12 muffins

Elizabeth's White Meal Cornbread

This is my mom's melt-in-the-mouth white meal cornbread. The finished cornbread freezes beautifully and, with a quick reheating, tastes fresh out of the oven.

Preheat oven to 450°   Spray 2 2-inch muffin tins with Pam.

2 cups White Lilly Brand Self-Rising Buttermilk
  Cornmeal Mix
2 Tbs. plain white flour
1/4 cup vegetable oil
1/2 cup buttermilk
1 cup water

1) Combine all ingredients in a medium mixing bowl and mix thoroughly with a wooden spoon. Pour into prepared tins and bake muffins 15-20 minutes. Turn on broiler at the end of baking to brown the tops of cornbread, if necessary.

Yields 12 muffins

Lemon Blueberry Muffins

Preheat oven to 425°

Grease 3 2-inch muffin tins
or 4 1-inch muffin tins

1 1/2 cup fresh or frozen blueberries
1/2 cup whole wheat flour
2 cups plain white flour
3/4 cup sugar
1 Tbs. baking powder
1/2 tsp. salt
1/2 tsp. cinnamon
2 eggs
1/2 cup milk
1/4 cup butter, melted and cooled
1/4 cup fresh lemon juice
1 tsp. grated lemon rind
2 Tbs. sugar for muffin tops

1) Rinse and drain blueberries. Pat dry.

2) Sift together all dry ingredients into a large mixing bowl. Add the blueberries and, tossing gently, distribute blueberries evenly throughout dry ingredients.

3) Whisk eggs lightly in a medium mixing bowl. Add milk, butter, lemon juice, and lemon rind. Whisk lightly until thoroughly blended.

4) Add egg mixture to dry ingredients and fold together with a rubber spatula until just blended. Do not over mix.

5) Spoon batter, being careful not to deflate, into prepared muffin tins. Sprinkle sugar over the tops. Bake in preheated oven for 20 minutes or until golden brown.

Makes approximately 15 2-inch muffins or 48 1-inch muffins.

Sweet Potato Muffins

Preheat oven to 425°   Grease 3 2-inch muffin tins
                                        or 4 1-inch muffin tins

1 1/2 cups plain white flour
1/4 cup whole wheat flour
1 cup sugar
2 tsp. baking powder
1/4 tsp. salt
1 tsp. cinnamon
1/4 tsp. nutmeg
1/4 cup raisins
1/4 cup chopped pecans
2 eggs
1/2 cup butter, melted and cooled
1 cup sweet potatoes, about 2 medium sized,
  baked, peeled, and mashed
1/2 cup milk
1/2 cup buttermilk
1/2 tsp. vanilla extract
1/2 tsp. fresh lemon juice

1) In a medium mixing bowl, combine both flours, sugar, baking powder, salt, cinnamon, nutmeg, raisins, and pecans. Blend thoroughly.

2) In a second mixing bowl, whisk together eggs, butter, sweet potatoes, milk, buttermilk, vanilla, and lemon juice.

3) Pour liquid mixture over dry ingredients and quickly fold together with a rubber spatula, being careful not to over mix. Entire mixing time should be about 5-7 seconds. Without any further stirring, spoon mixture into greased tins until each well is about 3/4 full.

4) Bake in preheated oven for 20-25 minutes or until muffins are golden brown.

Makes about 15 2-inch muffins or 48 1-inch muffins.

Applesauce Muffins
with Raisins and Pecans

Preheat oven to 425°

Grease 3 2-inch muffin tins
or 4 1-inch muffin tins

1 1/2 cups plain white flour
3/4 cup whole wheat flour
1 cup sugar
1 Tbs. baking powder
1/4 tsp. salt
1 tsp. cinnamon
1/4 tsp. nutmeg
1/4 cup raisins
1/2 cup chopped pecans
2 eggs
1/2 cup butter, melted and cooled
1 cup applesauce
1/2 cup buttermilk
1/2 tsp. vanilla extract
1/2 tsp. lemon extract

1) In a medium mixing bowl, combine both flours, sugar, baking powder, salt, cinnamon, nutmeg, raisins, and pecans.

2) In a second mixing bowl, whisk together eggs, butter, applesauce, buttermilk, vanilla and lemon extracts.

3) Pour liquid mixture over dry ingredients and quickly fold together with a rubber spatula, being careful not to overmix. Entire mixing time should be about 5-7 seconds. Without any further stirring, spoon mixture into greased tins until each well is about 3/4 full.

4) Bake in preheated oven for 15-20 minutes or until muffins are golden brown. Turn out onto rack to cool, or eat right away.

Makes about 15 2-inch muffins or 48 1-inch muffins.

Apricot Nut Bread
with Cream Cheese Spread

Preheat oven to 375°   Grease 1 5 x 9 inch loaf pan

1/2 cup dried, minced apricots
1/3 cup water
2 cups plain white flour
1 cup sugar
1 Tbs. baking powder
1/4 tsp. baking soda
3/4 tsp. salt
2 Tbs. butter, melted and cooled
1 egg, well beaten
1/2 cup orange juice
1 cup chopped pecans

1) Soak apricots in water for 20 minutes. Drain off water into orange juice. Set aside.

2) Sift together flour, sugar, baking powder, soda, and salt.

3) Add melted butter, egg, orange juice and water. Fold together lightly, working quickly. Stir in nuts and apricots.

4) Pour batter into prepared pan and bake 35-40 minutes or until center tests done with a toothpick. Remove from oven, allow to cool 10 minutes, then invert onto a rack and finish cooling. Serve with Cream Cheese Spread.

1 loaf

Cream Cheese Spread
6 ounces cream cheese, room temperature
2 Tbs. honey
1/3 cup finely chopped, dried apricots
1/3 cup chopped pecans

1) Combine all ingredients and blend thoroughly with a fork or wooden spoon.

Makes 1 cup

Elizabeth's Best Buttermilk Biscuits

Preheat oven to 450°

2 cups plain white White Lilly brand flour
1 1/4 tsp. salt
1/2 tsp. baking soda
1 Tbs. baking powder
1/2 cup + 1 Tbs. Crisco
1 1/3 cup buttermilk

1) In a medium mixing bowl, combine the flour, salt, baking soda, and baking powder. Mix thoroughly. Add the Crisco and work it into the flour with a pastry cutter until mixture is crumbly. Add buttermilk 1/2 cup at a time and mix thoroughly after each addition. After all milk has been added, stir vigorously for about a minute.

2) Turn dough onto a floured surface and knead lightly, adding flour, if necessary, to keep dough from sticking. After 4 or 5 kneads, dough should be a soft, smooth ball.

3) Roll dough out to a thickness of about 1/2 inch and cut with a 2-inch biscuit cutter. Lay biscuits on a cookie sheet, place in a preheated oven, and bake for 10 to 12 minutes. If necessary, run under broiler to brown tops.

Makes 24 two inch biscuits.

Desserts

The South has enjoyed a long-standing and well-deserved reputation as home to an abundance of outstanding desserts. Strawberry shortcake, pecan pie, and homemade pound cake are just a few of the classics intrinsically linked with our region and its cooks. My mother and grandmother embraced this tradition, perfecting their skills at an early age, and for their admiring and enthusiastic family produced an endless assortment of incredible sweets.

So, you can rest assured that a simple, unadorned bowl of fresh fruit never has been and never will be my idea of dessert. The preparation of imaginative and original sweets is my favorite aspect of cooking, and receives the highest priority in the Back Porch kitchen. We make everything from scratch, take few, if any, shortcuts, and use only the best ingredients available. I came by my sweet tooth honestly and it gives me great pleasure to be able to pass it on.

Matena's Almond Rum Torte

The recipe for this light as air, rum laced torte was shared with us by Matena Kalmer. It's a winner.

Preheat oven to 400°   Grease and flour 2 9-inch cake pans

6 egg whites, room temperature
1 cup sugar
1 1/2 cups toasted almonds, finely ground
  in food processor
1 Tbs. instant coffee
1 recipe Rum Syrup, recipe follows
1 recipe Whipped Cream Frosting,
  recipe follows
4 Tbs. toasted, sliced almonds for top

1) Place egg whites in a clean, dry, medium mixing bowl and beat with an electric mixer until soft peaks form. Add sugar a quarter cup at a time and continue beating until stiff, shiny peaks form. Fold in nuts and coffee with a rubber spatula until thoroughly blended.

2) Divide between two prepared cake pans, smoothing the tops and bake for 15-20 minutes or until center tests done with a toothpick. Invert tortes onto a kitchen towel dusted with confectioners sugar and allow to cool completely.

3) To assemble torte, place one layer on a decorative cake plate, brush generously with 1/2 of the Rum Syrup and cover with about 1/3 of the Whipped Cream Frosting.

4) Stack second torte layer on top, brush with remaining syrup, and cover top and sides with remaining Whipped Cream Frosting. Sprinkle sliced almonds over the top and serve well chilled

Serves 6-8

Rum Syrup
1/4 cup dark rum
1 Tbs. instant coffee

1) Mix together and set aside.

Whipped Cream Frosting
1 1/2 cups whipping cream, well chilled
1/4 cup sugar
1 Tbs. instant coffee
1 tsp. vanilla extract
1/4 cup toasted almonds, finely ground
*   in food processor*

1) Put chilled cream in medium mixing bowl and beat with an electric mixer until soft peaks form.

2) Add sugar, coffee, and vanilla and continue beating to a firm consistency. Fold in ground nuts. Keep well chilled.

Makes about 3 cups

Chocolate Raspberry Torte

Preheat oven to 325°   Grease and flour 1 12-inch cake pan

2 cups frozen raspberries, thawed
14 ounces bittersweet chocolate,
  chopped coarsely
1/4 cup water
8 ounces unsalted butter
6 egg yolks
1 1/3 cup sugar
9 Tbs. sifted cake flour
1 1/3 cup blanched almonds, ground fine in
  food processor
6 egg whites
1/2 tsp. cream of tartar
1 recipe Bittersweet Chocolate Glaze, see page 173
1 recipe Raspberry Sauce, see page 172

1) Put raspberries in bowl of food processor fitted with a steel blade and puree until smooth. This should make 1 cup of puree. Set aside.

2) Combine chocolate and water in a medium mixing bowl and set over a pot of simmering water. Stir occasionally. When chocolate has completely melted, remove from heat and whisk in butter, one tablespoon at a time, until chocolate is smooth and glossy. Set aside.

3) In another medium mixing bowl, combine egg yolks and sugar and beat with an electric mixer until pale yellow and very thick. Stir chocolate mixture into egg yolks and blend thoroughly. Add sifted flour and almonds and stir again until thoroughly blended. Then, add raspberry puree and blend thoroughly. Set aside.

4) In a clean, dry, medium mixing bowl beat egg whites until foamy with an electric mixer. Add cream of tartar and continue beating until stiff peaks form. Lightly fold egg whites into chocolate mixture in two additions, taking care to deflate the egg whites as little as possible.

5) Scrape batter into prepared pan, smooth the top and bake in preheated oven for about 35 minutes. Center may feel a little soft. Remove from oven and cool completely before inverting onto a decorative plate.

6) Glaze entire torte with Bittersweet Chocolate Glaze. Chill, then serve small wedges in pools of Raspberry Sauce. Top with whipped cream.

Serves 12-16

Chocolate Walnut Torte

Preheat oven to 375°

Grease and flour a
9-inch springform pan

8 ounces walnuts
1/3 cup sugar
6 ounces bittersweet chocolate,
  chopped fine
1 Tbs. grated orange rind
1/4 tsp. grated lemon rind
5 egg yolks
1/3 cup sugar
6 egg whites
1/2 tsp. cream of tartar
2 Tbs. confectioners sugar
2 ounces bittersweet chocolate, melted

1) In the bowl of a food processor fitted with a steel blade, combine walnuts and 1/3 cup sugar and grind until very fine. Transfer to a medium mixing bowl and add chopped chocolate, orange rind, and lemon rind. Toss to blend thoroughly. Set aside.

2) In another medium mixing bowl, combine egg yolks and 1/3 cup sugar and beat with an electric mixer until thick and pale yellow. Add chocolate walnut mixture and stir together until thoroughly blended. Mixture will be very stiff.

3) Place egg whites in a clean, dry mixing bowl and beat with an electric mixer until foamy. Add cream of tartar and continue beating until stiff peaks form. With a rubber spatula, very lightly fold a small amount of egg whites into chocolate walnut mixture to lighten the texture. Then, fold all remaining egg whites into mixture being very careful to deflate whites as little as possible.

4) Scrape batter into prepared pan and bake for 30 to 35 minutes or until springy to the touch in center. Remove from oven, allow to cool, and remove springform cuff. Transfer to a decorative platter, if desired. Sift powdered sugar over top of torte, then drizzle melted chocolate in a zig zag pattern over the top. Best served at room temperature.

Serves 6-8

Andy's Italian Cream Cake

This recipe, developed by friend and co-worker Andy Wilkerson, has become a Back Porch classic.

Preheat oven to 325°   Grease and flour 3 9-inch cake pans

4 ounces unsalted butter, room
 temperature
1/2 cup vegetable oil
2 cups sugar
5 egg yolks
1 tsp. baking soda
1 cup buttermilk
2 cups sifted, plain white flour
1 tsp. vanilla extract
2 tsp. orange liqueur
1 1/4 cups angel flake coconut
3/4 cup chopped walnuts
5 egg whites
1/2 tsp. cream of tartar
1 recipe Orange Cream Cheese
 Frosting, recipe follows

1) Combine butter, salad oil, and sugar in a medium mixing bowl and beat until fluffy with an electric mixer. Add egg yolks, one at a time, beating well after each addition.

2) Lightly stir baking soda into the buttermilk. Then add buttermilk, alternately with the flour, into the egg mixture, beating well after each addition.

3) Stir in vanilla, orange liqueur, coconut, and chopped walnuts. Set aside.

4) In a clean, dry mixing bowl, beat egg whites until foamy with an electric mixer. Add cream of tartar and continue beating until stiff peaks form. Lightly fold whites into batter in 2 additions, being careful to deflate the whites as little as possible.

5) Divide batter evenly between three prepared pans and bake for 40-45 minutes or until cake begins to pull away from the sides of the pan. Cool for 10 minutes before turning out of pan, then cool completely before frosting.

6) Frost cake between layers, on top and sides with Orange Cream Cheese Frosting and decorate with walnut halves and coconut, if desired.

Serves 10-12

Orange Cream Cheese Frosting
8 ounces cream cheese, room temperature
4 ounces unsalted butter, room temperature
1 pound sifted confectioners sugar
1/2 cup finely chopped walnuts
1 Tbs. orange liqueur
1 tsp. vanilla extract

1) In a medium mixing bowl, combine cream cheese, butter and confectioners sugar. Beat with an electric mixer until light and fluffy. Stir in walnuts, orange liqueur and vanilla until thoroughly blended.

Makes about 3 cups

Doris' Applesauce Date Nut Cake

This rich, moist, spice cake full of dried fruit and nuts has become a personal favorite, particularly in the cooler months. Though brought into our kitchen by Ruth Ann Toth, she gives full credit for the recipe to her mom, Doris Williams of Robersonville, NC. Thanks, Ruth and Doris.

Preheat oven to 325°   Grease and flour 1 large tube pan

8 ounces unsalted butter, room
  temperature
2 cups sugar
2 eggs
1 cup dates, chopped
1 cup raisins
2 cups walnuts or pecans, chopped
3 cups plain white flour
1/2 tsp. salt
2 tsp. baking soda
2 tsp. cinnamon
2/3 tsp. cloves
2 cups applesauce
1 recipe Cream Cheese Frosting
  optional, see page 174

1) Combine butter and sugar in a medium mixing bowl and cream thoroughly using an electric mixer. Add eggs and beat until light and fluffy.

2) Stir in dates, raisins, and nuts. Sift together flour, salt, soda, cinnamon, and cloves and add to mixture, stirring until thoroughly blended. Stir in applesauce. Batter will be very stiff.

3) Scrape batter into prepared tube pan and bake for 1 hour and 15 minutes or until cake tests done in the center with a toothpick. Allow to cool in pan for 20 minutes. Invert onto rack and cool completely. Dust lightly with sifted confectioners sugar or frost with Cream Cheese Frosting.

Serves 10-12

Frances' Fig Cake

There are many variations of fig cake being made on Ocracoke, but this one, brought into our kitchen by good friend and co-worker Frances O'Neal, is our favorite. If you want locally preserved figs, check the Community Store, where they sometimes have them for sale.

Preheat oven to 350°   Grease bundt pan with Crisco
                                        and dust with flour

3 eggs
1 1/2 cups sugar
1 cup vegetable oil
1/2 tsp. nutmeg
1/2 tsp. cloves
1 tsp. cinnamon
1 tsp. salt
2 cups plain white flour
1/2 cup buttermilk
1 tsp. baking soda, dissolved in 1 Tbs. water
1 tsp. vanilla extract
1 cup preserved figs, chopped
1 cup walnuts or pecans, chopped

1) In a medium mixing bowl, beat eggs until light and foamy. Add sugar and beat until pale and thick. Add oil and beat another minute.

2) Sift together nutmeg, cloves, cinnamon, salt, and flour. Add to eggs alternately with buttermilk beating well after each addition.

3) Stir in soda, dissolved in water, vanilla, figs and nuts.

4) Pour into prepared pan and place in preheated oven. Bake for 45 minutes or until cake tests done with a toothpick.

5) Cool in pan for 20 minutes then invert onto rack and cool completely. Transfer to serving plate and dust with confectioners sugar.

Serves 10-12

Andy's Chocolate Applesauce Cake

This spicy chocolate cake made with applesauce is a Back Porch favorite. We always try to make it a day or two ahead of time to give it time to ripen before serving.

Preheat oven to 350°   Grease and flour bundt pan

> *1/2 cup vegetable oil*
> *1 1/2 cups sugar*
> *2 eggs*
> *3 Tbs. cocoa, sifted*
> *3/4 tsp. cinnamon*
> *2 cups plain, white flour*
> *1 1/2 tsp. baking soda*
> *1/2 tsp. salt*
> *2 cups applesauce*
> *2 tsp. chocolate liqueur*
> *1 tsp. vanilla extract*
> *1 cup walnuts, chopped*
> *1 recipe Andy's Chocolate Sour Cream*
> *Frosting, recipe follows*

1) Combine oil and sugar in a medium mixing bowl and cream thoroughly. Add eggs, one at a time, beating well after each addition.

2) Sift together cocoa, cinnamon, flour, baking soda, and salt. Add to sugar and egg mixture in three additions, beating well after each.

3) Stir in applesauce, liqueur, vanilla, and nuts until just mixed.

4) Pour into prepared bundt pan and bake 30-40 minutes or until cake tests done with a tooth pick.

5) Cool in pan for 15 minutes before inverting onto a rack. Cool completely and frost with Andy's Chocolate Sour Cream Frosting.

Andy's Chocolate Sour Cream Frosting
3 ounces unsweetened chocolate
3 ounces semisweet chocolate
4 ounces unsalted butter, room temperature
1 cup sour cream
2 tsp. vanilla extract
1 Tbs. chocolate liqueur
5 cups sifted confectioners sugar

1) Melt chocolate in top of a double boiler. Remove from heat and cool completely.

2) In a medium mixing bowl, cream butter thoroughly. Add chocolate, sour cream, vanilla, liqueur, and sugar, and beat until light and fluffy.

Makes about 3 cups

Chocolate Hazelnut Cake

Our thanks go out to Cheryl Ballance for giving us this wonderful devil's food cake recipe. It was her family's favorite and we used it to create a spectacular three tiered wedding cake for her and her husband, Gene. We, serve it filled with mocha hazelnut buttercream and glazed in bittersweet chocolate.

Preheat oven to 350°   Grease and flour 2 9-inch cake pans

> *2 cups plain white flour*
> *2 cups sugar*
> *3/4 cup sifted cocoa*
> *1 tsp. baking powder*
> *2 tsp. baking soda*
> *1/8 tsp. salt*
> *2 eggs*
> *1/2 cup vegetable oil*
> *1 cup hot strong coffee*
> *1 cup milk*
> *2 tsp. vanilla*
> *1 recipe Mocha Hazelnut Buttercream, recipe follows*
> *1 recipe Bittersweet Chocolate Glaze, see page 173*

1) Place flour, sugar, cocoa, baking powder, baking soda, and salt in a medium mixing bowl and blend with a balloon whisk.

2) In a second mixing bowl, beat eggs with an electric mixer until foamy, add oil as you continue beating, then coffee, milk and vanilla.

3) Pour wet ingredients into dry and whisk together lightly with a balloon whisk. Pour into prepared pans and bake 35-40 minutes or until springy to the touch in the center. Remove from oven and allow to cool in pans for 10 minutes before inverting onto a rack to cool completely.

4) To assemble cake, put 1 totally cooled layer on a decorative plate. Spoon about 1/3 of Mocha Hazelnut Buttercream onto cake layer and smooth to the sides. Stack second layer on top and spoon another 1/3 of buttercream over top of cake. Smooth last 1/3 of buttercream into a thin layer on sides of cake. Refrigerate for 1 hour uncovered. Glaze entire cake with Bittersweet Chocolate Glaze and decorate top with whole hazelnuts, if desired. Store at room temperature.

Serves 12-16

Mocha Hazelnut Buttercream
1/2 cup egg whites, about 4
1 cup sugar
10 ounces unsalted butter, room temperature
2 Tbs. instant coffee
2 Tbs. brandy
1 tsp. vanilla extract
1 cup blanched, toasted hazelnuts
3 Tbs. confectioners sugar

1) Combine egg whites and sugar in a medium mixing bowl, whisk to blend thoroughly and place over a pot of simmering water. Stir slowly until mixture is warm to the touch and sugar is dissolved. Remove from heat and beat with an electric mixer on high speed until stiff peaks form. Beat on medium speed until mixture is room temperature.

2) Add butter to meringue 1 tablespoon at a time. With the last 2 additions of butter, buttercream will break, but will immediately be restored with continued beating.

3) Mix coffee, brandy and vanilla together in a small bowl and beat into frosting.

4) Put hazelnuts and confectioners sugar into the bowl of a food processor and process until nuts are finely ground. Fold nuts into buttercream.

Makes about 3 cups

Ruth Ann's Pound Cake

This is the only pound cake I ever make. I knew it was great, but imagine my satisfaction when my mom asked for the recipe. Given to me by Ruth Ann Toth and her mom, Doris Williams, this is a superlative, velvety, totally unforgettable version of the southern classic.

Preheat oven to 325°   Grease one large tube pan with
                                          Crisco and dust with flour

8 ounces unsalted butter, room temperature
1/2 cup Crisco
3 cups sugar
5 eggs, room temperature
3 cups Swansdown cake flour
1/2 tsp. baking powder
1 cup milk, room temperature
3 tsp. pure vanilla extract
1 1/2 tsp. pure almond extract

1) Combine butter and Crisco in a medium mixing bowl and beat until creamy and thoroughly blended. Add sugar and continue to beat until light and fluffy. Add eggs, one at a time, beating thoroughly after each addition.

2) Measure flour and baking powder, combine and sift three times. In a separate bowl, combine milk and extracts.

3) Mix flour and milk into butter mixture alternately in three parts, beginning and ending with flour. Beat thoroughly after each addition.

4) Pour batter into prepared tube pan and place in a preheated oven. Bake for approximately 1 1/4 hours or until cake tests done with a toothpick. Allow cake to cool in the pan for 20 minutes, run a thin knife blade around the sides, and lift cake out on center post. Cool completely, then remove from center post. Serve at room temperature with fresh berries and whipped cream.

Serves 10-12

Andy's Chocolate Brownies

Preheat oven to 350°

Lightly grease a 9 x 13 pan with Crisco and dust with flour

8 ounces unsalted butter
4 ounces unsweetened chocolate
2 cups sugar
3 whole eggs
1 tsp. vanilla extract
1/2 tsp. salt
1 cup plain white flour
1 cup chopped walnuts
1 Tbs. coffee liqueur
2 Tbs. confectioners sugar for top

1) Combine butter and chocolate in a small saucepan and melt over low heat. Whisk until smooth, remove from heat, and allow to cool to room temperature.

2) Stir in sugar, then beat in eggs, one at a time, with a wooden spoon.

3) Stir in vanilla, salt, and flour, until smooth, then walnuts and liqueur. Spread batter evenly into prepared pan.

4) Bake in preheated oven for 30-35 minutes or until center is set and brownies pull away from the sides of pan. Allow them to cool completely, then cut into 24 squares. Dust tops with confectioners sugar and remove from pan with a spatula.

Makes 24 one-inch squares

Flan

Over the years, we have served hundreds of these little jewels. Make small individual flans, as we do at the restaurant, or one large one.

Preheat oven to 325°   6 5-ounce tin molds or 1 5-cup souffle dish

3/4 cup sugar
1/4 cup water
4 eggs
1/2 cup sugar
dash salt
1 cup heavy cream
1 cup half and half
1 tsp. vanilla
1/2 gallon boiling water

1) Combine 3/4 cup sugar and 1/4 cup water in a small heavy bottomed saucepan. Stir to blend, then place over high heat. DO NOT STIR after mixture has been placed on heat. Cook, watching carefully, until mixture turns a rich amber color, then immediately pour into bottom of mold. Set aside to cool.

2) In a medium mixing bowl combine eggs, 1/2 cup sugar, salt, cream, half and half, and vanilla. Whisk until thoroughly blended. Pour into cooled, caramel lined mold.

3) Set mold in a 9 x 13 cake pan. Pour boiling water in pan until it comes about half way up the sides of mold. Cover mold with a pot lid or tray. This will keep tough skin from forming on top of custard during cooking.

4) Place in preheated oven and bake about 45 minutes for individual molds, 60 minutes for single mold. To test for doneness, give mold a nudge. Custard should give a firm jiggle.

5) Place mold on a rack to cool, then refrigerate overnight. To serve, invert custard onto a decorative plate allowing caramel syrup to run down the sides of custard.

Serves 6

Lemon Sponge Custard

Preheat over to 350°   6 6-ounce clear glass Pyrex custard cups

3/4 cup sugar
1 1/2 Tbs. unsalted butter, room temperature
1 Tbs. grated lemon rind
3 egg yolks
3 Tbs. plain white flour
1/3 cup fresh lemon juice
1 cup half and·half
dash salt
3 egg whites
1/4 tsp. cream of tartar

1) Combine sugar, butter, lemon rind, and egg yolks in a large mixing bowl and beat with an electric mixer until pale yellow.

2) Combine lemon juice and half and half and stir into above mixture, alternately with the flour. Stir in a dash of salt. Set aside.

3) In a clean, dry, mixing bowl beat egg whites until foamy, add cream of tartar, and continue beating until stiff peaks form. Fold into lemon mixture in 2 additions mixing until thoroughly blended.

4) Divide mixture evenly among 6 custard cups and place cups in a 9 x 13 cake pan. Pour hot water into the cake pan until it comes halfway up the sides of the cups.

5) Place in preheated oven and bake about 45 minutes. Tops should be nicely browned. Serve warm or chilled with whipped cream.

Serves 6

Creme Brulee

6 4-ounce ceramic ramekins

2 cups heavy cream
6 egg yolks
1/4 cup sugar
1 tsp. vanilla
6 Tbs. dark brown sugar for tops

1) Pour cream into a heavy saucepan and warm over low heat until almost simmering.

2) In a medium mixing bowl, whisk together yolks and 1/4 cup white sugar until thoroughly blended.

3) Pour 1/2 cup hot cream into yolks, beating constantly, then pour warmed yolks back into cream in saucepan. Watching carefully and stirring constantly with a rubber spatula, cook over medium low heat until very hot and nicely thickened. (Note: Should mixture curdle from over heating, cool slightly, then process for 1 or 2 minutes in food processor. If mixture is not severely over cooked, this will usually restore it nicely). Remove from heat and stir in vanilla.

4) Fill ramekins to the brim and place, uncovered, in the refrigerator. After a couple hours, cover with saran wrap, then allow to chill 8 hours or overnight.

5) About 1 hour before serving, remove from refrigerator, unwrap, and place on a tray. Smooth about 1 Tbs. dark brown sugar on the top of each custard. Run under a broiler, watching carefully, until sugar has liquefied into a crusty caramel top. Return to refrigerator and serve within 2 to 3 hours.

Serves 6

Fruit Creme Brulee

This is a great midsummer variation on the classic Creme Brulee. We use strawberries or peaches, feeling that a naturally tart fruit works best.

4 6-ounce clear glass Pyrex cups

1/2 cup sugar
1/4 cup water
1 generous cup sliced strawberries or peaches
dash cinnamon
1 recipe Creme Brulee completed through step 3,
  see page 138

1) In a small saucepan, combine sugar and water and cook over medium heat until sugar is dissolved and mixture is boiling.

2) Put fruit in medium mixing bowl and pour sugar syrup over it, stirring to blend. Add a dash of cinnamon. Divide fruit and syrup equally between 4 custard cups.

3) Add a dash of cinnamon to the brulee custard and divide it equally between the 4 cups by gently floating it on top of the fruit. Dust the tops with a sprinkle of cinnamon. Refrigerate for 8 hours or overnight before serving.

Serves 4

Back Porch Apple Bread Pudding

We prepare our apple bread pudding using leftover applesauce muffins, but any kind of sweet muffin or spice cake could be used.

Preheat over to 325°   Generously butter a 6-cup, straight sided, souffle dish and line the bottom with buttered parchment paper

2 Tbs. butter
3 Granny Smith Apples, peeled, cored
  and sliced
2 Tbs. sugar
12 1-inch muffins, approximately,
  sliced crosswise
2 Tbs. brandy
4 eggs
1/2 cup sugar
1 cup half and half
1 cup whipping cream
1 tsp. pure vanilla extract
1 tsp. brandy
dash salt
dash cinnamon
dash nutmeg
1/2 gallon boiling water
1 recipe Caramel Sauce, see page 171

1) In a large sauté pan, heat butter, then add the apple slices. Sauté, tossing frequently, until soft and slightly brown. Sprinkle with 2 Tbs. sugar and continue cooking until nicely browned. Remove from heat.

2) Line bottom of mold with half the apples arranged in concentric circles, then layer half the muffin slices over the apples. Sprinkle muffins generously with half the brandy. Repeat with remaining apples, muffins, and brandy.

3) In a medium mixing bowl, whisk together eggs, sugar, half and half, cream, vanilla, brandy, salt, cinnamon, and nutmeg. Pour mixture over apples and muffins.

4) Place pudding in a 9 x 13 pan and place on center rack in oven. Pour boiling water into pan until it comes about a third of the way up the side of souffle dish. Cover souffle dish with a flat lid. Bake for 1 1/2 hours, approximately. Custard should be firmly set throughout.

5) Remove pudding from pan and set on a rack to cool, then chill overnight before serving. To serve, invert onto a decorative plate, being sure to remove the circle of parchment paper. Surround with a generous pool of Caramel Sauce and pipe rosettes of whipped cream on the top.

Serves 8-10

Chocolate Bread Pudding

Try this recipe with leftover banana bread - it's great.

Preheat oven to 325°   Butter a 6 cup, straight sided, souffle dish and
                        line the bottom with buttered parchment paper

> *6 ounces bittersweet chocolate, chopped*
> *1 cup half and half*
> *1 cup whipping cream*
> *20 1-inch muffins, sliced crosswise*
> *3 Tbs. brandy*
> *5 eggs*
> *1/2 cup sugar*
> *1 tsp. vanilla*
> *1 tsp. brandy*
> *dash cinnamon*
> *1/2 gallon boiling water*
> *1 recipe Creme Anglaise, see page 173*

1) Combine chocolate, half and half, and cream in a medium sized mixing bowl set over a pot of simmering water. When cream is very hot and chocolate is soft, whisk until smooth, remove from heat and set aside to cool.

2) Meanwhile, stack sliced muffins into three layers in buttered souffle dish, sprinkling each layer generously with brandy.

3) In a medium mixing bowl, whisk together eggs, sugar, vanilla, brandy, and cinnamon. Whisk in the cooled chocolate mixture. Pour mixture over muffins.

4) Set pudding in a 9 x 13 cake pan and place on the middle rack of a preheated oven. Fill cake pan with boiling water, and cover the pudding with a flat lid. Bake for about 1 hour. Remove lid and bake another 20-30 minutes until set throughout.

5) Remove pudding from cake pan and place on a rack to cool, then refrigerate overnight. To serve, run a thin knife blade around the edge of the mold and invert pudding onto a decorative plate. Peel off parchment paper, surround with a pool of Creme Anglaise and pipe rosettes of whipped cream on top.

Serves 8-10

Poached Figs with Sherry Sabayon

Mid-July through August is harvest time on Ocracoke for the local fig crop. We have several large trees in our yard at home and when I get tired of putting up preserves, I fix this dessert for the dining room.

20 whole, fresh figs
4 Tbs. fresh lemon juice
10 paper thin slices of lemon, seeds removed
1 cup brown sugar
1 Tbs. dry sherry
1 recipe Sherry Sabayon, recipe follows

1) Rinse figs, leave whole, and place in a shallow saucepan. Add lemon juice, lemon slices, brown sugar, and sherry, and just enough water to barely cover figs. Cook slowly over low heat until the figs are soft and the liquid is syrupy. Place all in a bowl and refrigerate overnight.

2) To assemble, remove figs from the syrup and cut in half lengthwise. Place 5 halves on each dessert plate in a star burst pattern with the stem ends meeting in the center. Spoon a little syrup over the figs. Put a generous spoonful of Sherry Sabayon in the center and garnish with whipped cream and mint leaf.
Serves 8

Sherry Sabayon
8 egg yolks
3/4 cup sugar
1/2 cup sherry
1/4 cup dry Chablis
1/2 cup whipping cream

1) Combine egg yolks, sugar, sherry, and Chablis in a medium mixing bowl, whisking thoroughly. Place over a pot of simmering water and, whisking constantly, cook until mixture is very thick and bright hot.

2) Remove bowl from heat and immediately place in another bowl of ice water. Whisk mixture occasionally until cold. Set aside.

3) Pour whipping cream in a small mixing bowl and whip until soft peaks form. Fold cream into the chilled sabayon until thoroughly blended. Store in refrigerator.
Makes 3 cups

Lemon Mousse in Tulip Shells

This is one of the showiest desserts we do and also one of the most complicated. We recommend staggering the preparation over two days. Prepare the base for the mousse and the crepe shells the first day; finish the mousse, fry the shells and prepare the sauce the second day. If you can find frozen crepe shells at your specialty food store, don't hesitate to use them.

> *2 cups sugar*
> *12 egg yolks*
> *1 cup lemon juice*
> *8 ounces unsalted butter, cut into 16 pieces*
> *2 Tbs. grated lemon rind*
> *1/2 cup egg white*
> *1/4 tsp. cream of tartar*
> *2 Tbs. sugar*
> *1/2 cup whipping cream*
> *2 cups vegetable oil for frying crepe shells*
> *1 recipe Crepe Shells, see page 182*
> *1 recipe Blueberry Sauce, see page 172*

1) In a heavy non-aluminum saucepan combine sugar, egg yolks, and lemon juice and whisk until smooth. Place over low heat and cook, stirring constantly until mixture is thick and almost to a boil.

2) Remove from heat and immediately stir in butter 4 pieces at a time, allowing each addition to melt completely before adding the next. Stir in lemon rind. Chill thoroughly, preferably overnight, before proceeding.

3) To finish mousse, beat egg whites until foamy, add cream of tartar, and continue beating until soft peaks form. Add sugar and beat until stiff peaks form. Fold whites into chilled lemon mixture with a rubber spatula. Set aside.

4) Whip cream until soft peaks form. Fold cream into lemon mixture and refrigerate until serving time.

5) To fry crepes, either preheat a deep fryer to 350° or heat 2 cups vegetable oil in a heavy bottomed saucepan, watching carefully. To test temperature of oil for readiness, pinch a tiny bit of crepe and throw into oil. When it sizzles and floats, proceed.

6) Lay crepe on top of hot oil, place bowl of small ladle in the center and partially submerge crepe to form a small cup. Hold in this position until lightly browned and crispy. Turn over to brown the tops, then remove to a paper towel and cool.

7) To assemble, place fried crepe shell on dessert plate, fill with Lemon Mousse and spoon Blueberry Sauce over the top. Garnish with dollop of whipped cream and a mint leaf.

Serves 8-10

Poppy Seed Parfait

Spray the insides of 7 5-ounce metal or glass molds with Pam

1/2 cup poppy seeds
1 cup milk
2 Tbs. honey
1 packet unflavored gelatin
1/4 cup water
5 egg yolks
1/2 cup sugar
1 cup whipping cream
1 tsp. vanilla extract
1 recipe Raspberry Sauce, see page 172
1 recipe Creme Anglaise, see page 173

1) Put poppy seeds on a cookie sheet and toast in a preheated 375° oven for 25-30 minutes, shaking the pan at regular intervals. Poppy seeds should have a strong roasted aroma and taste when finished. Set aside to cool.

2) Combine milk and honey in a heavy saucepan over low heat and warm until film forms on top.

3) Combine gelatin and water in small bowl and set aside.

4) Combine egg yolks and sugar in a medium mixing bowl and whisk until thoroughly blended. Slowly add scalded milk, stirring constantly. Return mixture to saucepan and cook over low heat, stirring constantly, until mixture thickens and is almost to a boiling point. Remove from heat and add softened gelatin. Whisk to blend and dissolve gelatin. Set saucepan in a bowl of iced water and stir mixture until cool and thick, but not set. Remove and set aside.

5) Pour whipping cream into a deep mixing bowl and whip until soft peaks form. Add vanilla and continue to beat until firm peaks form. Add cooled custard and poppy seeds and mix together until thoroughly blended, using a whisk or mixer, if necessary.

6) Spoon mixture into prepared molds and level the tops with a knife. Cover and refrigerate overnight.

7) To assemble, ladle a half moon of Raspberry Sauce and a half moon of Creme Anglaise onto individual dessert plate, allowing the two sauces to meet in the middle. Run a thin knife blade around the inside of the mold to loosen parfait and invert onto plate. Top with whipped cream and mint leaf.

Serves 7

Chocolate Mosaic

This is for chocolate lovers only. To my taste, the aroma of the brandy, the tartness of the fruit, and the rich, bittersweetness of the chocolate are a winning combination.

Spray a 7 x 13 inch loaf pan with Pam and line completely with parchment paper, cut to fit. Spray again.

1/3 cup golden raisins, chopped fine
1/3 cup dried apricots, chopped fine
1/3 cup dried pineapple, chopped fine
1 tsp. grated orange rind
1/4 cup brandy
1 1/2 cups whipping cream
12 ounces bittersweet chocolate, chopped fine
1/3 cup toasted hazelnuts, coarsely chopped
1 recipe Brandy Creme Anglaise, recipe follows
1 recipe Orange Gel, recipe follows

1) Combine dried fruits, orange rind and brandy in a medium mixing bowl and set aside for 2 hours.

2) Heat cream in a heavy saucepan, add chocolate, and whisk until smooth. Remove from heat and place in a bowl of cool water continuing to stir until chocolate is cool and thickened but not set.

3) Stir in fruit with brandy and hazelnuts and pour into prepared pan. Refrigerate overnight.

4) To assemble, pour a pool of Brandy Creme Anglaise into individual dessert plates. Drop Orange Gel into cream in a decorative pattern. Invert chocolate loaf onto a cutting board and remove parchment paper. With a hot, wet knife, gently slice 1/4 inch thick portions and lay in pool of sauce.

Serves 10-12

Brandy Creme Anglaise
1 cup milk
5 egg yolks
1/4 cup sugar
dash salt
1/2 tsp. vanilla
1 Tbs. brandy

1) Pour milk in medium saucepan and warm over low heat until film forms on top.

2) In a medium mixing bowl, combine egg yolks, sugar, and salt and whisk until smooth. Slowly add scalded milk, stirring constantly, then return to saucepan.

3) Cook mixture over medium heat, stirring constantly, until slightly thickened. Remove from heat, add brandy and vanilla, and allow to cool. Chill thoroughly before using.

Makes about 2 cups

Orange Gel
1 cup fresh squeezed orange juice, strained
2 tsp. cornstarch
2 tsp. orange liqueur

1) Pour orange juice into medium saucepan and heat to a simmer.

2) Combine cornstarch and orange liqueur and pour into juice, stirring until thickened. Remove from heat and chill.

Makes about 1 cup

Bittersweet Chocolate Terrine

This is undoubtedly our best selling chocolate dessert of all time and with good reason. If you're looking for a simple preparation that yields impressive results, this recipe can't be beat. We have developed three different presentations. The first calls for baking and serving the chocolate in a 4-ounce ramekin garnished with whipped cream and toasted nuts. The two fancier presentations allow the custard to be removed from the ramekin and inverted into a pool of sauce surrounded by fresh fruit.

Preheat oven to 325°   7 4-ounce ceramic ramekins

> 6 ounces bittersweet chocolate, chopped
> 1 cup half and half
> 1 cup whipping cream
> 2 Tbs. sugar
> 6 egg yolks
> 1 1/2 Tbs. hot brewed coffee
> 2 Tbs. instant coffee
> 1 tsp. vanilla
> 1/2 gallon boiling water

1) Combine chocolate, half and half, cream, and sugar in a bowl set over a pot of simmering water. Heat until chocolate is melted and mixture is smooth when whisked. Break egg yolks into a second medium mixing bowl. Combine brewed coffee, instant coffee, and vanilla in a small bowl.

2) Whisk 1 cup of hot chocolate mixture into the egg yolks, then pour warmed yolks back into chocolate mixture and cook for another minute, stirring constantly with a rubber spatula. Remove from heat and stir in coffee and vanilla.

3) Fill ramekins with chocolate and set them in a 9 x 13 cake pan. Pour enough boiling water in the pan to come halfway up the sides of the ramekins. Cover with a lid. Place in a preheated oven and bake for 35-40 minutes, leaving chocolates semisoft in the center. Remove from oven, allow to cool, and chill overnight.

4) To serve, place ramekins on a dessert plate and top them with a spoonful of whipped cream and a sprinkling of chopped toasted nuts.

Serves 7

Bittersweet Chocolate Terrine
in White Chocolate Sauce with Strawberries

7 4-ounce ramekins sprayed with Pam

1/2 cup cocoa
1 recipe Bittersweet Chocolate Terrine, see page 150
  completed through step 2
1 recipe White Chocolate Sauce, see page 171
1 cup fresh strawberries, hulled, rinsed, and diced fine
7 whole strawberries for garnish

1) Dust sprayed ramekins with light coating of cocoa, so chocolates will release when inverted.

2) Fill ramekins with chocolate and cook according to directions for Bittersweet Chocolate Terrine. Chill overnight.

3) To assemble, ladle a pool of White Chocolate Sauce into dessert plate. Run a thin knife blade around terrine to loosen, then invert into your hand. Place terrine in center of sauce and spoon chopped strawberries into sauce around terrine. Place whole strawberry and rosette of whipped cream on top.

Serves 7

Bittersweet Chocolate Terrine
in Caramel Sauce with Fresh Fruits

7 4-ounce ramekins sprayed with Pam

1/2 cup cocoa
1 recipe Bittersweet Chocolate Terrine, see page 150,
  completed through step 2
1 recipe Caramel Sauce, see page 171
1 1/2 cup diced mixed fruit, we use kiwis,
  peaches, and strawberries

1) Dust sprayed ramekins with light coating of cocoa, so chocolates will release when inverted.

2) Fill ramekins with chocolate and bake according to directions for Bittersweet Chocolate Terrine. Chill overnight.

3) To assemble, ladle a pool of Caramel Sauce into dessert plate. Run a thin knife blade around terrine to loosen, then invert into your hand. Place terrine in center of sauce and spoon mixed fruit into sauce around terrine.

Serves 7

Pear Normandy Tart

Preheat oven to 300°   1 9-inch pie pan

1 partially baked walnut Ground Nut Crust, see page 169
4 ounces cream cheese, room temperature
2 Tbs. sugar
1/4 cup whipping cream
1 egg yolk
1/4 tsp. vanilla
1/4 tsp. fresh lemon juice
1/2 tsp. grated lemon rind
dash nutmeg
dash salt
5 ripe pears, D'anjou or Bartletts
2 Tbs. clarified butter
2 Tbs. sugar
2 tsp. fresh lemon juice
1 tsp. cornstarch, optional
1 tsp. water, optional
1/2 recipe Sugar Crumb Topping, see page 170

1) Cream 4 ounces cream cheese and sugar until smooth. Beat in whipping cream, egg yolk, vanilla, lemon juice, lemon rind, nutmeg, and salt. Smooth into the bottom of partially baked walnut crust. Bake in preheated 300° oven for 8-10 minutes until filling is barely set around edges.

2) Meanwhile, peel, quarter, and core the pears. Slice the quarters crosswise into thin pieces. Heat 2 Tbs. clarified butter, add the pear slices, and saute, tossing frequently, until pears are thoroughly soft and beginning to brown. Add sugar and lemon juice. If pears have released their juices and mixture contains a lot of liquid, combine cornstarch and water and stir into mixture. Return to a simmer and stir until thickened.

3) Spoon pears, with all their cooking juices, over cream cheese filling. Sprinkle a half recipe of Sugar Crumb Topping over the top of pie. Increase oven temperature to 375° and bake pie for 35 to 40 minutes or until topping is lightly browned and crispy. Serve slightly warm.

Serves 6-8

Dried Apple Tart with Molasses

Preheat oven to 350°   1 10-inch tart pan

> *1 partially baked pecan or walnut*
> *Ground Nut Crust, see page 169*
> *12 ounces dried apples*
> *4 cups water*
> *3 Tbs. butter*
> *1 1/2 cup molasses*
> *3/4 tsp. grated lemon rind*
> *1 1/2 Tbs. fresh lemon juice*
> *1 pinch nutmeg*
> *1/4 cup granulated sugar*
> *1/2 recipe Sugar Crumb Topping, see page 170*

1) In a medium sized saucepan, combine apples and water, bring to a boil and simmer for 6 or 7 minutes. Drain, reserving 3/4 cup of the water.

2) Return apples, 3/4 cup reserved water, butter, molasses, lemon rind, lemon juice, nutmeg, and sugar to saucepan and cook slowly over low heat, stirring often.

3) When apples appear translucent and dark brown in color and when syrup has thickened and reduced to about 1/2 to 3/4 cup, remove pot from heat and allow contents to cool. Apples can sit overnight at this point and will continue to plump, absorbing molasses syrup.

4) Pour apples into prepared crust, distribute evenly, and scatter Sugar Crumb Topping over the fruit. Bake in preheated oven until bubbly around edges and crispy and brown on top.

Serves 8-10

Apple Crumb Tart

Preheat oven to 375°   1 10-inch tart pan

> *1 partially baked pecan*
>   *Ground Nut Crust, see page 169*
> *5 or 6 Granny Smith apples, peeled,*
>   *cored, and sliced*
> *2 Tbs. flour*
> *3/4 cup sugar*
> *dash of cinnamon*
> *1 tsp. grated lemon rind*
> *1 Tbs. fresh lemon juice*
> *1/2 recipe Sugar Crumb Topping, see page 170*

1) In a large bowl, combine apples, flour, sugar, cinnamon, lemon rind, and lemon juice. Toss well to coat apples.

2) Arrange apple mixture in pecan crust and sprinkle Sugar Crumb Topping over the fruit.

3) Place tart on cookie sheet lined with foil and bake in preheated 375° oven for 55 minutes or until fruit is bubbling throughout and topping is nicely browned.

Serves 6-8

Chocolate Apricot Almond Tart

Preheat oven to 350°   1 10-inch tart pan

1 partially baked almond
  Ground Nut Crust, see page 169
3/4 cup sugar
1 1/2 cup sliced, blanched almonds
4 1/2 Tbs. apricot preserves, pureed
  in food processor
3/4 cup whipping cream
3 Tbs. amaretto liqueur
2 dashes salt
2 ounces bittersweet chocolate

1) In a medium mixing bowl, combine sugar, almonds, apricot preserves, cream, amaretto, and salt. Blend thoroughly and pour into prepared crust.

2) Bake in preheated oven for 30-35 minutes, remove from oven and allow to cool.

3) Melt 2 ounces chocolate in top of double boiler and drizzle over cooled pie in a zig zag pattern. Serve warm with whipped cream.

Serves 8-10

Peach, Raspberry and Orange Crumb Tart

Preheat oven to 375°   1 10-inch tart pan

1 partially baked pecan Ground Nut Crust, see page 169
3 to 4 cups peaches, peeled and sliced
1 cup raspberries, fresh or frozen
1 navel orange, peeled, juicy sections
  cut away from connecting tissue, see page 187
1 tsp. grated orange rind
3/4 to 1 cup sugar, to taste
3 to 4 Tbs. flour
1/2 recipe Sugar Crumb Topping, see page 170

1) In a medium mixing bowl, combine peaches, raspberries, orange sections, orange rind, sugar, and flour. Mix thoroughly and pour into prepared crust.

2) Scatter Sugar Crumb Topping over fruit and place tart on cookie sheet lined with foil. Bake in preheated oven for about 45 minutes or until fruit is bubbling throughout and topping is nicely browned. Serve slightly warm with whipped cream.

Serves 6-8

Chocolate Strawberry Pie

This pie requires a lengthy chilling, so prepare it early in the morning or a day ahead of time.

1 9-inch pie pan

1 1/4 cup graham cracker crumbs
3 Tbs. sugar
1/3 cup melted butter
8 ounces cream cheese, room temperature
1/4 cup light brown sugar
1/2 tsp. vanilla extract
3 ounces bittersweet chocolate, melted and cooled
1 cup whipping cream
1 cup sliced strawberries
2 ounces bittersweet chocolate
1 tsp. unsalted butter

1) For crust, blend graham cracker crumbs, sugar, and 1/3 cup melted butter in a medium mixing bowl. Press into bottom and around sides of a 9-inch pie pan. Chill.

2) In a medium mixing bowl, combine cream cheese, brown sugar, and vanilla and beat until light and fluffy. Stir in melted chocolate blending thoroughly.

3) In a separate bowl, whip heavy cream until soft peaks form and fold cream into chocolate mixture. Pour into prepared crust and chill at least 8 hours.

4) Just before serving, cover top of pie with sliced strawberries, arranged in overlapping, concentric circles.

5) Melt 2 ounces bittersweet chocolate with 1 tsp. unsalted butter and drizzle over the strawberries in a zig zag pattern.

Serves 6-8

Sweet Potato Pie

Preheat oven to 350°   1 9-inch pie pan

1 partially baked walnut
  Ground Nut Crust, see page 169
1 1/2 cups sweet potatoes, about 2 medium
  sized, baked, peeled and mashed
1/2 cup light brown sugar
1 Tbs. white sugar
3 whole eggs
1/2 cup whipping cream
1/4 cup melted butter, cooled
1/4 tsp. nutmeg
1/4 tsp. cinnamon
1/4 tsp. salt or a little more to taste
1/2 tsp. vanilla extract

1) Whisk together sweet potatoes and all remaining ingredients in a medium mixing bowl. Taste and correct seasonings.

2) Pour into prepared crust and bake 40-45 minutes or until filling is set throughout. Serve warm with whipped cream.

Serves 6-8

Lola's Pecan Pie

This pecan pie recipe, given to me by my grandmother, is without equal. The light corn syrup, the vinegar, and the finely chopped pecans give this version of the southern classic its refinement and distinction.

Preheat oven to 350°   1 9-inch pie pan

>*1 partially baked Basic Pie Crust, see page 168*
>*3/4 cup light corn syrup*
>*3/4 cup white sugar*
>*3 whole eggs*
>*4 Tbs. melted butter*
>*1 Tbs. white vinegar*
>*1 pinch salt*
>*1 tsp. vanilla extract*
>*1 1/2 cups finely chopped pecans*

1) In a medium mixing bowl combine corn syrup, sugar, eggs, butter, vinegar, salt, and vanilla. Whisk thoroughly. Stir in pecans.

2) Pour mixture into pie crust and bake 40-45 minutes or until set throughout and golden brown. Serve at room temperature with whipped cream.

Serves 6-8

Elizabeth's Coconut Pie

This superior coconut pie recipe, developed by my mom, is the only coconut pie we ever make.

Preheat oven to 350°   1 9-inch pie pan

> 1 partially baked Basic Pie Crust, see page 168
> 1 1/2 cups sugar
> 2 Tbs. flour
> 5 eggs
> 3/4 cup butter, melted and cooled
> 1/2 cup buttermilk
> 2 cups angel flake coconut
> 1 tsp. vanilla

1) Combine sugar, flour, and eggs in a medium mixing bowl and whisk thoroughly. Stir in butter, buttermilk, coconut, and vanilla.

2) Pour mixture into crust and bake about 35-40 minutes or until set throughout and golden brown. Remove from oven, cool slightly, and serve warm with whipped cream.

Serves 6-8

Lime Curd Tart in Almond Crust

This flavorful fruit curd can be made with lemons or limes. It is the foundation for many outstanding desserts, however, this simple lime curd tart is our favorite.

1 10-inch tart pan

1 fully baked almond Ground Nut Crust, see page 169
2 cups sugar
12 egg yolks
1 cup fresh lime juice
2 Tbs. grated lime rind
1/2 pound unsalted butter, cut into 16 equal pieces

1) Combine sugar, yolks, and lime juice in a heavy stainless steel or enamel saucepan, whisking thoroughly. Place over medium heat and, stirring constantly with a rubber spatula, cook until thick and bright hot, but not boiling.

2) Remove from heat and immediately stir in lime rind and butter pieces, one at a time.

3) Pour directly into fully baked pie crust and chill several hours or overnight. Garnish with whipped cream rosettes and lime slices if desired.

Serves 8

Lemon Cream Cheese Tart
in Pecan Crust with Blueberries

Preheat oven to 350°   1 10-inch tart pan

1 partially baked pecan Ground Nut Crust, see page 169
3 cups blueberries, fresh or frozen
1/3 cup sugar
2 tsp. cornstarch
2 tsp. water
8 ounces cream cheese, room temperature
1/3 cup sugar
1/4 cup fresh lemon juice
5 whole eggs
1 tsp. grated lemon rind
3/4 cup whipping cream
dash salt

1) In a medium saucepan, combine blueberries and sugar and cook over medium heat until berries release their juices and the mixture is boiling. Dissolve cornstarch in water and pour into berries, stirring constantly, until mixture has returned to a boil and is slightly thickened. Set aside to cool.

2) In a medium mixing bowl, beat cream cheese until light and creamy. Add sugar and lemon juice and beat until smooth. Then add eggs and beat until thoroughly blended. Stir in lemon rind, cream, and salt.

3) Set the partially baked pie crust on the middle rack of a preheated oven. Pour filling into shell. It will be quite full. Close oven door and bake tart for 30 minutes or until just set. Remove from oven and allow to cool. Spoon blueberries over the top of tart and smooth to the edges. Serve chilled with whipped cream.

Serves 6-8

Chocolate Amaretto Cheesecake

1 9-inch springform pan

1 cup chocolate cookie crumbs
1/3 cup graham cracker crumbs
1/4 cup sugar
3 ounces melted butter
5 ounces bittersweet chocolate, chopped coarsely
2 ounces unsalted butter
2 1/2 pounds cream cheese, room temperature
1 cup sour cream
1 1/4 cup sugar
3 ounces amaretto liqueur
1 tsp. almond extract
6 eggs

1) Combine chocolate cookie crumbs, graham cracker crumbs, sugar, and melted butter in a medium mixing bowl. Toss thoroughly and press into the bottom of a 9-inch springform pan. Set aside.

2) Combine chopped chocolate and 2 ounces unsalted butter in the top of a double boiler and heat until thoroughly melted and smooth. Remove from heat and set aside.

3) In a large mixing bowl, beat the cream cheese until light and fluffy. One at a time, beating well after each addition, add the sour cream, sugar, amaretto, and almond extract. Add eggs and beat until just blended.

4) Pour batter into prepared pan and swirl in chocolate mixture with a rubber spatula. Put pan on a cookie sheet, then place in a cold oven. Turn oven to 325° and bake for approximately 1 1/2 hours. When done, cake will be slightly puffed and will jiggle firmly when nudged. Remove from oven, allow to cool, then refrigerate overnight before serving.

5) To serve, run a thin knife blade around inside of cuff to loosen. Remove cuff and cut cake into wedges with a hot, wet knife.

Serves 10-12

Lemon Pecan Cheesecake

1 9-inch springform pan

1 1/2 cups graham cracker crumbs
1/4 cup sugar
3 ounces melted butter
1 1/4 cups pecans, chopped
2 ounces butter
2 1/2 pounds cream cheese, room temperature
1 cup sour cream
1 1/2 cups sugar
grated rind of 1 1/2 lemons
3/4 cup fresh lemon juice
6 eggs

1) For crust, combine graham cracker crumbs, 1/4 cup sugar, and melted butter in a medium mixing bowl. Toss thoroughly and press into the bottom of a 9-inch springform pan. Set aside.

2) Heat 2 ounces butter in a large sauté pan, add pecans, and toss to coat with butter. Watching carefully and tossing frequently, cook pecans until toasted on all sides. Set aside to cool.

3) In large mixing bowl, beat cream cheese until light and fluffy. One ingredient at a time, mixing well after each addition, add sour cream, sugar, lemon rind, and lemon juice.

4) Add toasted pecans, including all the browned butter in the pan. Add all the eggs and mix until just blended. Pour into prepared springform pan.

5) Place pan on a cookie sheet and put in a cold oven. Turn heat to 325° and bake for approximately 1 1/2 hours or until cake is slightly puffed and firm when nudged. Remove from oven, allow to cool, then refrigerate overnight before serving.

6) To serve, run a thin knife blade around inside of cuff to loosen. Remove cuff and cut cake into wedges with a hot, wet knife.

Serves 10-12

Almond Apricot Swirl Cheesecake

This recipe was developed in the Back Porch kitchen by my sister, Peggy, before she moved on to bigger and better things. Whenever we miss her, which is often, we make this wonderful cheesecake in her honor.

1 9-inch springform pan

1 1/2 cups graham cracker crumbs
1/4 cup sugar
3 ounces melted butter
3/4 cup dried apricots
1 cup water
2 Tbs. brandy
1 Tbs. fresh lemon juice
1/4 cup sugar
2 1/2 pounds cream cheese, room temperature
1 cup sour cream
1 1/4 cup sugar
1 1/2 cups toasted almonds, ground fine in
*   food processor*
1 1/4 tsp. vanilla extract
1 1/4 tsp. almond extract
6 eggs

1) For crust, combine cracker crumbs, sugar, and melted butter in a medium mixing bowl. Toss thoroughly and press into the bottom of a 9-inch springform pan. Set aside.

2) In a small saucepan, combine apricots and water. Simmer, covered, until apricots are soft. Put apricots and all the cooking liquid, in the bowl of a food processor, along with brandy, lemon juice, and 1/4 cup sugar. Puree until smooth and set aside.

3) In a large mixing bowl, beat cream cheese until light and fluffy. One ingredient at a time and beating well after each addition, add sour cream, sugar, ground almonds, vanilla, and almond extract. Add all the eggs and mix until just blended.

4) Pour batter into springform pan and swirl in apricot puree with a rubber spatula.

5) Put pan on cookie sheet then place in a cold oven. Turn oven to 325° and bake for about 1 1/2 hours. When done, cake will be slightly puffed and browned and will jiggle slightly when nudged. Remove from oven, allow to cool, and refrigerate overnight before serving.

6) To serve, run a thin knife blade around inside of cuff to loosen. Remove cuff and cut cake into wedges with a hot, wet knife.

Serves 10-12

Basic Pie Crust

This buttery, flaky crust recipe makes enough for 2 single crust pies or 1 double crust pie. Unused dough stores well in refrigerator or freezer. Note: In this book, I define 1-10 inch tart pan as a shallow, straight sided, 10-inch ceramic or metal pan; and 1 9-inch pie pan as a deep, slant sided, 9-9 1/2 inch ceramic, glass, or metal pan.

3 cups plain white flour
1 tsp. salt
1 cup chilled Crisco
3 Tbs. chilled unsalted butter
6 Tbs. water

1) Sift flour and salt into a medium mixing bowl. Add half the Crisco and half the butter and work into flour with a pastry cutter until mixture resembles coarse meal. Work in second half Crisco and butter until mixture resembles small peas.

2) Add water and toss mixture lightly with a fork until evenly moistened. Turn onto a lightly floured board, press mixture into a smooth mound, and divide dough into two equal parts. Wrap pieces separately and refrigerate for 1 hour.

3) Remove first piece of dough from refrigerator, place on lightly floured board and press with hands into a 5-inch disc. Then, using a rolling pin, roll out into a thin sheet slightly bigger than your pan. Roll sheet around rolling pin to pick up and transfer to pan. Smooth pastry into pan, crimp edges, and trim excess. Repeat with second piece of dough.

4) To prebake, cut a 10-inch square of waxed paper, spray one side with Pam, then smooth paper into crust, sprayed side down. Fill with 2 cups dried beans or rice, place in a preheated 350° oven and bake for 7-10 minutes. Remove from oven, remove wax paper and beans, and return to oven for an additional 3 or 4 minutes. The edges should be just beginning to brown and the bottom should be slightly puffy and dry to the touch. Finish with desired filling and proceed according to recipe directions.

Yields 2 crusts

Debbie's Ground Nut Crust

This crust is so handy, we keep the raw crumbs on hand in the refrigerator at all times. Note: In this book, I define 1 10-inch tart pan as a shallow, straight sided, 10-inch ceramic or metal pan; and 1 9-inch pie pan as a deep, slant sided, 9-9 1/2 inch ceramic, glass, or metal pan.

Preheat oven to 350°   Spray pan with Pam

> *3 cups plain white flour*
> *1/2 cup sugar*
> *10 ounces nuts - almonds, pecans, or*
> * walnuts, finely ground in food processor*
> *1 pinch nutmeg*
> *1/2 tsp. grated lemon rind*
> *1/2 pound butter, cut into small pieces*
> *1 Tbs. honey or molasses*
> *1 whole egg*
> *1 tsp. vanilla extract*

1) Combine all ingredients and using hands, pastry cutter, or dough hook in counter top mixer, blend until mixture forms moist crumbs with all ingredients evenly distributed.

2) Press crumbs into bottom and around sides of pan and bake until top edge is just beginning to brown. Freeze remaining crumbs.

Yields 2 crusts

Sugar Crumb Topping

1/4 pound butter, chilled
1 cup plain white flour
1 cup sugar

1) Place all ingredients in medium mixing bowl and blend with a pastry cutter until all ingredients are evenly distributed and fine moist crumbs are formed.

2) Scatter 1/2 of the crumbs over top of pie and bake at 375° until topping is lightly browned and crispy. Store remaining crumbs in airtight container in refrigerator or freezer for up to two weeks.

Yields enough for 2 pies

White Chocolate Sauce

5 ounces white chocolate, chopped
1 cup whipping cream
1/2 tsp. vanilla extract

1) Combine white chocolate and cream in a medium saucepan and set over low heat. Warm gently and whisk until smooth. Stir in vanilla and chill before using.

Makes about 1 1/2 cups

Caramel Sauce

1/2 cup granulated sugar
1/4 cup water
3/4 cup heavy cream

1) Combine sugar and water in a small saucepan and place over high heat. Do not stir. Cook, watching carefully, until color is deep amber.

2) Immediately begin to add cream in amounts of 1 Tbs. at a time, stirring constantly. (Caramel will foam and harden around cream, but will become smooth as the cream warms.) When all the cream has been added, return to a full boil, and remove from heat. Serve warm or chilled. Chilled sauce will be thicker.

Makes about 1 cup

Raspberry Sauce

2 cups frozen raspberries, thawed
1 cup sugar
1 Tbs. fresh lemon juice

1) Combine all ingredients in bowl of food processor and process for 2 minutes.

2) Force sauce through fine strainer with a rubber spatula to remove seeds. Chill before serving.

Makes about 2 cups

Refrigerate or freeze

Blueberry Sauce

2 cups fresh or frozen blueberries
1/2 cup sugar
1/2 cup water
1 tsp. cornstarch
1 tsp. water

1) In a medium saucepan, combine blueberries, sugar, and 1/2 cup water over medium heat and bring to a boil. Reduce heat to a gentle simmer and cook until berries have released their juices and sugar is dissolved.

2) Mix cornstarch and 1 tsp. water together until smooth. Add to blueberries, stirring constantly, until mixture has returned to a simmer and thickened slightly.

3) Cool and serve as is, or cool and strain, pressing on solids to extract all juice.

Makes about 1 1/4 cups

Creme Anglaise

1 cup milk
5 eggs yolks
1/4 cup sugar
dash salt
1/2 tsp. vanilla extract

1) Place milk in a medium sauce pan and warm over medium heat until a film forms on top.

2) In a separate bowl, whisk together egg yolks, sugar, and salt.

3) Slowly add the hot milk to egg mixture, whisking constantly, then immediately return mixture to sauce pan.

4) Stir gently over low heat until slightly thickened. Remove from heat and stir in vanilla. Chill thoroughly before serving.

Makes about 1 1/2 cups

Bittersweet Chocolate Glaze

4 ounces unsweetened chocolate
2 ounces unsalted butter
2 cups sifted confectioners sugar
5 Tbs. boiling water

1) Melt chocolate and butter together in a medium mixing bowl set over simmering water. Whisk until smooth.

2) Remove from heat. Add sifted sugar and water and whisk until smooth and glossy. Use immediately.

Enough to glaze the outside of 1 cake or torte

Cream Cheese Frosting

8 ounces cream cheese, room temperature
4 ounces unsalted butter, room temperature
1 tsp. vanilla extract
1 pound confectioners sugar, sifted

1) Combine all ingredients in a medium mixing bowl and beat until light and fluffy.

Enough for one 9-inch, 2 layer cake

Whipped Cream

1 cup whipping cream
6 Tbs. sugar
1 tsp. vanilla extract

1) Pour whipping cream into a medium mixing bowl and set in freezer for 5 minutes.

2) Remove cream from freezer and, with an electric mixer, beat vigorously until soft peaks form. Add sugar and vanilla and beat until slightly firm peaks form. Store well chilled.

Makes about 1 1/2 cups

Basics and Helpful Tips

Clarified Butter

8 ounces salted or unsalted butter

1) Heat butter in sauce pan until bubbly. Remove from heat and set aside for 1 hour while all milky particles settle to the bottom.

2) With a ladle, skim the melted butterfat into another container, leaving milky residue in bottom of sauce pan. Discard milky residue. Butter fat is now clarified and ready to use.

Yields about 1 cup clarified butter

Andy's Herbed Champagne Vinegar

This vinegar is so special, I urge everyone to try it. It's well worth the wait.

24 2-inch rosemary sprigs
20 peeled garlic cloves
1 1/2 cups golden raisins
1/2 gallon Champagne vinegar or any other
  good quality white wine vinegar.

1) Cut herbs early in the morning before the sun hits them. Rinse and pat dry.

2) Put rosemary sprigs, garlic cloves, raisins, and vinegar into a 1/2 gallon jar. Seal tightly.

3) Place the vinegar on a sunny porch or window sill for 4 weeks to infuse.

4) After 4 weeks, strain vinegar, discarding solids.

5) Fill decorative glass bottles with strained vinegar, adding a sprig of fresh rosemary and 6 or 7 golden raisins to each. Will keep for 1 year.

Yield 8 cups

Herbed Chevre

I'm especially fond of fresh chevres and have found that marinating them in herbs and olive oil is a good way to preserve their freshness. Use this recipe as a guide and come up with your own combinations.

8 ounces fresh chevre
1/2 cup or more virgin olive oil
1/2 tsp. dried rosemary leaves
1/2 tsp. dried basil leaves
1 tsp. fresh, minced garlic

1) Slice chevre into 1/2 inch thick discs or slices and place in a plastic container for which you have a tight fitting lid. Mix the oil, herbs, and garlic together. Pour over the cheese, making sure it is completely covered with oil. Store in refrigerator for up to a month. Use in salads, on Herbed Chevre Croutons, or spread on crackers.

Herbed Chevre Croutons

Preheat oven to 400°

Any amount of Herbed Chevre
Any amount of French bread, cut into thin slices

1) Spread Herbed Chevre generously onto slices of French bread. Toast in preheated oven for 3-5 minutes, or until bread is crispy and cheese is soft and warm. Serve with soups, salads, or alone, as a light snack.

Homemade Buttered Croutons

Preheat oven to 425°

4 cups French bread, cut into 1/2 inch cubes
3 ounces clarified butter

1) Scatter bread cubes evenly on cookie sheet and place in preheated oven. Toast until lightly browned and crispy.

2) Using a ladle, drizzle butter evenly over toasted bread cubes. Toss bread cubes and return to oven.

3) Continue to toast until thoroughly crisp and golden brown. Remove from oven, cool thoroughly, and store in airtight container.

Dry Bread Crumbs

Preheat oven to 325°

Any amount of any kind of bread ends, excluding
sweet tasting muffins or breads

1) Place bread ends on cookie sheet and toast in oven until dry and crispy, but not overly browned. Run bread ends through food processor fitted with a steel blade until fine crumbs result. Store in a plastic bag in the freezer indefinitely.

Crepe Shells

1 cup plain white flour
2/3 cup milk
2/3 cup water
3 eggs
1/4 tsp. salt
3 Tbs. melted butter
additional 1/2 cup melted butter, if necessary

1) Measure flour into medium bowl. Whisk in milk and water until smooth. Beat in eggs, salt, and butter. Let batter sit for at least 2 hours before frying.

2) Heat small 8-inch frying pan or crepe pan, until drops of water sizzle in the pan. Lightly brush pan with additional melted butter. (A well seasoned pan will only require this for the first 1 or 2 crepes.)

3) Pour 2 or 3 tablespoons batter into the center of pan, turning pan in all directions to evenly spread batter into a thin pancake. Cook for 30 seconds or until edges are nicely browned, then turn over with a thin spatula and cook 10-15 seconds more.

4) Slide crepe out of pan onto a rack to cool and repeat with remaining batter. Do not allow crepes to become brittle in the open air. When cool, cover immediately.

About 15 crepes

Rice

The only rice we use at the Back Porch is Ellis Stansel's Gourmet Rice. It is shipped to us weekly from Gueydan, Louisiana, where Mr. Stansel has 260 acres under cultivation. Be forewarned - once you've tasted Ellis Stansel's rice, you'll never be satisfied with anything else. To order your own 10 pound bag write to:

Ellis Stansel's Gourmet Rice
P.O. Box 206
Gueydan, Louisiana 70542
(318) 536-6140

2 1/4 cups water
1/2 tsp. salt
1 cup Ellis Stansel's Gourmet Rice
1 Tbs. butter

1) Combine water and salt in a small saucepan and bring to a boil over high heat. Add rice and stir. Return to a boil. Reduce heat to a simmer, cover, and cook 20 minutes or until all moisture is absorbed. Remove from heat, stir in butter, cover, and let rice sit another 5-7 minutes. Serve immediately.

Makes about 3 cups

Pesto

2/3 cup fresh basil leaves, firmly packed
1 tsp. minced fresh garlic
1/3 cup blanched almonds
1/3 cup olive oil
1/3 cup grated parmesan cheese
1/4 tsp. salt
1/2 tsp. freshly ground black pepper

1) Place basil leaves, garlic and almonds in the bowl of a food processor. Process until finely ground.

2) With the processor still running, add the oil in a steady stream until completely blended.

3) Stop the processor and add the cheese, salt and pepper. Process until just blended. Set aside.

Yields about 1 cup

Peeled, Seeded and Chopped Tomatoes

Bring a pot of water to a boil, add tomatoes and leave for 30 seconds. Drain off water and allow tomatoes to cool. Skins will slip right off. (Use same process to skin peaches.) Slice in half crosswise, give tomatoes a slight squeeze, and the seeds will pop right out. Discard seeds and skin. Chop remaining tomato as desired.

Sun Dried Tomatoes

We use a lot of sun dried tomatoes at the Back Porch and find the really tasty ones that come packed in olive oil hard to locate, expensive to buy, and difficult to ship. Follow these instructions and end up with the same thing.

> *Any amount sun dried tomatoes, the type that*
> *comes packed in bags. Halves or whole*
> *tomatoes work better than slices*
> *Water*
> *Salt*
> *Any good quality vegetable oil or olive oil.*

1) Place dried tomatoes in a medium sauce pan and barely cover with water. Sprinkle generously with salt, and simmer for 30-45 minutes or until tomatoes are soft and water is almost absorbed. Drain tomatoes completely, allow to cool, and chop coarsely. Put in clean glass jar and cover completely with oil. Store in refrigerator.

Toasted Nuts

Place nuts on a cookie sheet and put in a 350° oven. Bake until lightly browned throughout, watching carefully, and tossing frequently. Allow to cool completely.

or

Heat 2 Tablespoons clarified butter in large skillet. Add nuts and cook, watching carefully and tossing frequently, until browned on all sides. Allow to cool.

Blanched Nuts

Blanched nuts refers to any nut with the outer skin removed, most commonly peanuts and almonds, and, more recently, hazelnuts. I try to purchase all my hazelnuts already blanched, but when I can't, this is how I remove their black bitter skins.

Bring 3 cups of water to a boil, add 4 Tablespoons baking soda, then 1 cup hazelnuts. Boil nuts about 3 minutes. To test for doneness, run one nut under cold water. Skin should slip right off. If not, boil a little longer. When done, rinse under cold water and separate nuts from skins. Dry the nuts and place on a cookie sheet. Roast in a 350° oven until well browned and crispy. Watch carefully.

Citrus Sections

This simple technique for extracting citrus sections works great on grapefruits, oranges, lemons, or limes.

Using a very sharp knife, cut both ends off of fruit deep enough to expose juicy sections. Then, setting fruit on counter with a cut end down, slice peeling off in strips, cutting deep enough to expose juicy sections and remove all white membrane. You should now have totally peeled fruit, free of all white peeling. Insert a thin knife blade between the sections and their connective tissues and release the juicy sections intact. Hold fruit over a bowl to collect juice. Remove seeds, if any. Resulting sections should be free of all white membrane, connecting tissue and seeds.

Skinning Fish

To skin a raw fish fillet, lay fillet on smooth counter or cutting board with the length of the fish facing you. Place fillet fairly close to the edge of the counter. Hold a sharp, long bladed knife in right hand, hold the fish at very base of the tail with left hand. Insert knife just above your fingers, right at the tail of the fish. Insert knife to, but not through, the skin, and lay the blade almost flat against the counter. With your left hand, begin to work the skin back and forth under the blade as you begin to pull. With your right hand, move the blade gently back and forth along the length of the fillet. The skin should come right off in one piece.

Cutting Herbs and Scallions

To cut fresh herbs or scallions, one needs either a very sharp knife or a pair of scissors.

Dill, parsley, sage, rosemary, oregano and cilantro can all be minced on a cutting board without risk of bruising or discoloring. Basil, chives, and scallions need to be handled carefully and either snipped with scissors into small pieces or sliced with a very sharp knife and used immediately.

Blanching Vegetables and Greens

We blanch a lot of vegetables and greens at the Back Porch using the following method.

Bring a large pot of water to a boil. Fill another large pot with ice and water. Plunge prepared vegetables into boiling water and, watching carefully, cook to desired doneness. Vegetables should retain bright color and crisp texture for maximum appeal and nutrition. When done, immediately drain off all water, then plunge vegetables into iced water. Leave until completely chilled. Drain again. Vegetables are now ready to use.

Index